21 Days, Steps & Keys

The Complete Book Series to Better Balance

Edited by Beth Wallace & Elizabeth (Bette) Frick, PhD, ELS

Cover design and layout by Lukas J. Dickie

Back cover photo by Richard Yates

Printed by CreateSpace

Distributed by Creative Consulting

Find more copies of this book online at
21complete.com

ISBN 978-0-9854503-7-3
10 9 8 7 6 5 4 3 2 1

21

Days
Steps
& Keys

The Complete Book Series

to Better Balance

Michael Thomas Sunnarborg

For my nieces, Nicolette & Natalie.

*In honor of all writers, coaches, and people
finding their passion and voice. Keep on.*

Preface

> *Life isn't about finding yourself.*
> *Life is about creating yourself.*
> George Bernard Shaw

My search for better balance began while I was living in Honolulu, Hawaii, in the 1990s. A good friend and I were making observations about how the mind, body, and spirit are connected. We discussed how our life experience reflected our state of balance; the more balanced we were, the more serenity and peace we felt. As time passed, I began to document the observations and insights I was experiencing, and 15 years later the books began to appear.

In my first book, *21 Days to Better Balance*, I introduced 21 themes to help readers connect with themselves and find more balance in their mind, body, and spirit. Book two, *21 Steps to Better Relationships*, helped readers strengthen their relationships and find more balance with others. The third book, *21 Keys to Work/Life Balance*, brought the concept of integration—rather than separation—to understanding the delicate balance between our lives and careers. This book contains the entire text of all three books.

Balance is a natural state. Returning to better balance means removing the barriers to balance within us, many of them created by our own thoughts and behaviors. My books, blogs, coaching and speaking engagements highlight the guiding principles that have had the largest impact on my ability to find more balance and harmony in my life. Sometimes the best teacher is our own experience.

My hope is that the personal observations, insights, and stories I've used to help find better balance in my life will help you find better balance in yours.

To your best balanced life!

Michael Thomas Sunnarborg

September 2014

Introduction

The human brain naturally searches for patterns. A common theme in all three of my books is the number 21. This number was derived from the premise for the first book, which is based on the notion that it takes 21 days to make or break a habit. Rather than writing in a typical narrative style, I chose to divide the guiding principles into 21 bite-sized portions; this felt more palatable and easier to digest. Subsequently, the theme of "21" resonated as the foundation for books two and three.

The books contain three chapters, each focusing on one of the three steps of awareness, alignment, and activation. Each chapter leads you through seven themes outlining the balance process. Along with the themes, some chapters contain exercises to help reinforce that stage of development. At the end of each theme are questions for a Balance Plan and either an Affirmation, Call to Action, or Key Actuator:

📖 Balance Plan questions	Daily Affirmation
✋ Call to Action	Key Actuator

You might find it useful to journal about the Balance Plan questions, or simply mull them over during your day. They can also serve as a useful meditation focus; simply bring the question into your mind during your regular meditation practice and notice the thoughts that float up in response. Repeating the affirmations can help you internalize the lessons from each day. You might post them on your bathroom mirror or computer monitor. I know one person who posts each day's affirmation in the middle of her car's steering wheel so that she remembers it on the way to work and on her way home.

The Call to Action and Key Actuator are "to-do" activities designed to help you apply the lessons from each theme. Putting theory into practice helps integrate the concepts into your experience.

The themes are progressive and will be best-understood if read in order—at least the first time through. Then after you've completed the book you can return to any of the themes or exercises to refresh yourself as needed.

The content in this book is very direct. If any of the introductory text feels overwhelming, try skipping down and reading the analogy or story before re-reading the larger messages. This may help you set the appropriate context for the daily theme.

These books will help you create a Balance Plan. The plan is meant to help you apply the insights contained in this book. Plan templates are included in the *21 Days, Steps & Keys Workbook*, or you can make your own. The plans are meant to help you apply the insights contained in the books. Start by thinking of a current problem or situation in your life where you'd like to create better balance—for example, your job, your finances, or a relationship—and use the plan to document your answers to the daily questions. Your plan can help shed light on the situation and support you in brainstorming potential solutions.

Let's get started!

Book One

21 Days to Better Balance

Find More Balance in a Busy World

Introduction

It takes 21 days to make or break a habit. Over the next 21 days, I'm going to lead you through a three-step process of awareness, alignment, and activation designed to gently shift your perspective, remove barriers, and help you find better balance in your mind, body, and spirit. At the end of the process, you will have established new habits that will help to keep you moving in the direction of a balanced life.

Throughout this book I will be associating the mind with *thoughts*, the body with *feelings*, and the spirit with *intuition*. These associations help to identify how you might experience your mind, body, and spirit in more tangible ways.

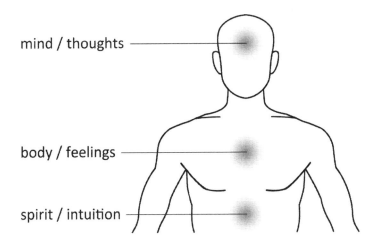

Remember: The power to make changes in your life is *always* in your hands. Make a commitment to start paying closer attention to your thoughts, feelings, and intuition and create the momentum for better balance in your life today.

Chapter 1: Welcome to Awareness

Let us not look back in anger, nor forward
in fear, but around in awareness.
James Thurber

Humans are multi-sensory beings. Our powerful consciousness is absorbing and processing everything in our environment—sights, sounds, and smells—whether we realize it or not. In order to find better balance in our lives, we must first become aware of the factors that influence our balance.

The next seven days will be spent taking a closer look at awareness. Raising our awareness helps us reconnect with our natural state of balance and reminds us that the power to change our lives is always in our hands.

Day 1: Thoughts

Awareness

> *The ancestor of every action is a thought.*
> Ralph Waldo Emerson

Thoughts are most often associated with logic, cognition, reasoning, and the mind. The mind is the source of our thoughts. Although the mind is a complex and vast resource of knowledge, memories, and perceptions—a metaphorical scrapbook of our life experiences—it is not our thoughts. Thoughts are only energetic vibrations created in the mind. But in the process of creating, thoughts are powerful tools.

All thoughts contain energy. When you think a thought, you send out an energetic signal, and that signal produces an effect. As the thought process continues, the energy around the thought will grow and begin to manifest in your experience. Whatever you pay attention to will expand. Have you ever thought about someone and then seen or heard from them shortly afterward? Have you gone to sleep with a problem and woken up with a solution? These are examples of how powerful our thoughts can be.

Our thoughts are affected by everything that we encounter, and we have the power to sort, prioritize, and control our thoughts. When we take control of our thoughts, we can choose which thoughts to focus on—we can literally *change our minds*. When we change our thoughts, we will change our experiences. We are in control.

Being aware of your thoughts allows you to choose them and control their power.

Thoughts are like advertisements. Each day we are bombarded by a variety of messages designed to bring us information and persuade us to take some sort of action. But most of us only take action on a small percentage of advertisements.

We have the ability to tune out advertisements by turning off the radio or TV, putting down the newspaper, or simply choosing to ignore the message. We are in control.

Similarly, each day we entertain thoughts bringing us information and persuading us to believe something or take some sort of action. But for the most part, we only take action upon a small percentage of the thoughts we think. Just as with advertisements, we can decide how to respond to our thoughts. We have the option to accept or dismiss a thought, choose a new thought, or slow down our thoughts through relaxation activities such as deep breathing or meditation. Again, we are in control.

How do your thoughts help you today? Where do your thoughts get in your way? How have your thoughts been helpful or harmful in your current situation?

How could a shift in your thinking help you to support yourself in a healthier way?

I am able to control my thoughts and choose to focus only on those thoughts that serve me.

Day 2: Feelings

*I've learned that people will forget what you said,
people will forget what you did, but people will
never forget how you made them feel.*
Maya Angelou

Feelings are experienced as responses in the body—for example, we may experience happiness, joy, excitement, and love as a quickened heartbeat, a burst of energy, or warmth in the area of our heart. Similarly, confusion, disappointment, anger, and hate may show up as a clenched jaw, a knot in the stomach, or a weight on our shoulders. Feelings can be invoked through external events like watching a film, winning a contest, smelling a familiar smell, or through internal triggers like thoughts or memories.

As with thoughts, we have the power to choose how we communicate our feelings. Being able to identify, control, and express feelings in a healthy way takes time, patience, and practice, but it will always—*always*—bring us into better alignment with our thoughts and intuition. Expressed feelings can bring relief or resolution. Unexpressed feelings can bring pain and/or manifest as disease or addictions.

Like thoughts, feelings also have an energetic frequency and directly affect behavior. Feelings are much easier to observe in others than are thoughts. We can pick up on other people's feelings through the inflection of their words, their body language, and their facial expressions.

**Being aware of your feelings helps you
to balance your emotional well-being.**

Feelings are like a thermometer—an indicator of our emotional state of being. Much like taking our body temperature, stopping to take our "emotional temperature" helps us to measure and monitor our feelings. When our feelings are affecting our thoughts or behaviors, we may feel "hot" with anger or "cold" with depression.

We are out of alignment when our behavior is out of line with our true feelings.

Whenever your emotional temperature is fluctuating, stop and ask yourself, "How am I feeling?" "What is causing these feelings?" and "How can I respond to my feelings in a healthy way?" Stopping to identify your feelings and their sources gives you the opportunity to understand them and figure out how to process them. As with your body temperature, sometimes it takes time to rebalance your emotional temperature. With patience and understanding, you can return to a state of better emotional balance.

How have your feelings played a role in your current situation?

If your current situation were ideal, how would you feel?

I am aware of my feelings and able to respond to them in healthy ways.

Day 3: Intuition

> *We are not human beings on a spiritual journey.*
> *We are spiritual beings on a human journey.*
> Stephen R. Covey

Intuition is the language of our spirit—a connection to God, Source Energy, Creator, the Divine, the Universe, or whichever name you use to describe a power greater than any one of us. The voice of our intuition is quiet and often difficult to hear. We can become aware of our intuition by taking the time to listen to our thoughts, acknowledge our feelings, and create a space for our intuitive voice to be heard.

Many of us interpret the voice of our intuition through a nudge or a hunch associated with a "gut" feeling—different and deeper than a typical emotional response. We all have been given intuition, although many of us have not been taught how to use it. Much like developing a muscle, strengthening intuition takes practice and patience.

The first step is learning to trust our intuition. Intuition is the voice of our spirit—our soul and higher consciousness—and it will always contain our deepest truth. Even though we may not be able to explain immediately why something does or doesn't feel right, we can learn to allow intuition to play a critical role—along with our thoughts and feelings—in the decision making process.

Being aware of your intuition helps
provide clarity and confirmation
of your thoughts and feelings.

Intuition is like a compass. If we are hiking in unmarked territory and get lost, a compass gives us feedback about our current position in relationship to North. With this knowledge, we can reset our course with confidence and return to our journey.

Our intuition is a spiritual compass. If we pay attention to it, it can help us find and maintain our direction. Taking time to check with our intuition gives us feedback that either validates our direction or helps us correct our course. Our intuition will always point to our inner truth—our true North.

When have you had an intuitive nudge about a decision or situation? How did you receive or act on your intuition? How did it turn out?

How could following your intuition bring better balance to your current situation?

**I recognize that my intuition is a gift
and I am learning to trust it.**

Day 4: Frequency

*Quantum physics has found that there is no
empty space in the human cell, but it is a teeming,
electric-magnetic field of possibility or potential.*
Dr. Deepak Chopra

Everything that exists in our physical reality contains atomic particles; therefore, everything we observe has an energetic frequency. Objects that are mobile—such as humans and animals—appear to be "alive" since we observe their movements. Immobile objects, such as rocks, don't appear to be alive but still have an energetic frequency. Frequency is the source of all physical form and everything we observe is vibrating at some level.

Our personal frequency is extremely sensitive. We don't have an "off switch," but we do have a rheostat that allows us to adjust our own vibrations. As with feelings, we are able to observe the frequency of others by the inflection of their words, body language, and facial expressions. We might refer to these observations as good or bad "vibes." Our personal frequency is highly influenced by other people. Our energetic response to others can be a source of valuable information if we are aware of it.

**Being aware of your frequency allows you to
notice how people and environments affect you.**

Personal frequency is like a radio station. Every radio station is unique. Each station has a different channel and different programming and plays different music. Higher frequencies aren't any better than lower ones; they're just different. For example, 101.5 isn't a better radio station than 98.3; it just plays different music. Similar to radio stations, each person has individual thoughts, feelings, and perspectives. We are tuned in to our own frequency and broadcasting our own music to the world through our being.

When we meet people whose frequency is similar to ours, we tend to connect with them easily—we say we're "on the same channel." Being around people whose frequency is different from ours may cause us to feel awkward or uncomfortable.

Even though we may experience the "higher" or "lower" frequencies of others, none of us is better than anyone else; we're just different. Honoring a variety of frequencies gives us the opportunity to appreciate others, just like listening to new and different music.

How has the intersection of your frequency with the frequency of others contributed to your current situation?

In what ways might raising awareness of your frequency assist you in your current situation?

**I am aware of my frequency
and how it affects my balance.**

Day 5: Fear
Awareness

> *Courage is fear that has said its prayers.*
> Dorothy Bernard

Fear is an essential part of the human experience. Fear itself does not have power—it is what we associate with fear that gives fear strength. Fear is just a signal to pay attention to something—and paying attention to our fear takes courage and commitment.

The physiological roots of fear are meant to protect us from danger or injury. The body reacts to the feelings triggered by fear—such as panic, confusion, or anger—with the "fight or flight" response. This reaction is a natural animal instinct that originates in the primitive brain. What sets us apart from animals is our ability to reason and control our behaviors. As human beings, we have the potential to stop, think, and *respond* to fear instead of merely reacting to it. When we are afraid, reacting without thinking only allows fear to trigger us into unconscious and often destructive behaviors.

Fear gives us the opportunity to learn about ourselves. Ignoring fear doesn't make it go away—it only returns with more ferocious power. Facing fear means shining the light of understanding on what is currently in the dark. When we face our fear, we have the opportunity to heal and to learn from it. Unresolved fear can manifest within us as stress, frustration, and self-doubt. Overcoming our fear gives us back our strength and confidence.

Being aware of your fear creates opportunities
for continued healing and personal growth.

Fear is like a fire alarm. When a fire alarm goes off, it may startle us, but there is no reason to panic or become upset. Reacting to a fire alarm with fear can interrupt our ability to think clearly and rationally.

The alarm is meant to prompt us into responding with appropriate action—in this case, vacating the building. Imagine what would happen if we ignored a fire alarm or became hysterical and, indeed, the building was on fire. Signals are sent for a reason.

Similarly, when fear sets off an alarm inside us, we are being prompted to take action. Ignoring the alarm doesn't make it go away. Bringing attention to the object of our fear allows us to take action, face our fear, and learn from the experience.

How has your fear influenced your current situation? What fears do you hold about changing the situation?

How can approaching your fear with courage, joy, and love effect the outcome?

I understand that fear is only a signal, and I have the courage to face my fear and learn from it.

Day 6: Time

Awareness

> *The secret of health for both mind and body is not*
> *to mourn for the past, worry about the future,*
> *or anticipate troubles, but to live in the*
> *present moment wisely and earnestly.*
> Buddha

Time is a measurement—a marker to remember where we've been, notice where we are, and imagine where we are going. Time is a human construct. Human beings have created time to help us understand the relationships between events.

Time can be categorized as chronological, emotional, or spiritual. Chronological time keeps track of events by clock and calendar. Emotional time describes the ways that time can shift depending on our feelings. Spiritual time marks the beginning and end of a process that's related to our personal growth and development as a unique individual being.

Time can be fluid. Directing our thoughts creates our reality in the present moment. The imagination can allow us to move beyond physical time and project thoughts into the past, present, or future. When we are focused on the future, time appears to slow down. When we are focused on the past, time appears to speed up. When we focus on the present moment and enter into a state of energetic flow, time can expand and appear to stop completely. Accepting time as fluid releases us from the need to control time.

Being aware of time allows you to honor
and respect the timing of all things.

Time is like money. Physical dollars and coins have no *real* value, only the value we assign to them or perceive them to have. We spend money in exchange for an item or an experience we want. Similarly, we receive money in exchange for things or actions. Giving and receiving money is an energetic transaction.

24

Time, like money, is temporary—once we've spent those dollars or minutes, they are gone. How we choose to spend them is up to us. Think of the words we assign to how we spend our time and money—for example, we can waste either time or money. Time spent with others can be considered "priceless." Money can be invested, and so can time—for example, by spending an afternoon with a grandparent. Time, like money, is a perceived construct and a critical marker in our experience.

Have you been focusing on the past, present, or future with regard to your current situation?

How could an effective use and understanding of time help you to effect positive change?

**I am aware of time and respect the value
of spending it wisely and thoughtfully.**

Day 7: Flow

> *As your faith is strengthened, you will find that*
> *there is no longer the need to have a sense of control,*
> *that things will flow as they will, and that you will*
> *flow with them, to your great delight and benefit.*
> Emmanuel Teney

Being in a state of flow—or what I like to call "in the zone"—is a state of conscious connection with a stream of creative energy. A state of flow comes from a direct connection to spirit, the basis for the word *inspiration*. When we are in the zone, our creative energies move to us and through us with simplicity and ease. Thoughts and ideas come quickly and easily, and our creativity is expressed through our actions and words. This flow can be experienced during any type of activity, whether it is physical, intellectual, emotional, or spiritual. We can be in the zone and receiving its benefits as long as we are able to establish and maintain our focus.

The state of flow can be initiated in many ways. Intimate engagement—the act of focusing on the details of a task, situation, event, or person—allows for a deeper connection with our spirit. By releasing control, we allow ourselves to be literally *out of our minds* and connected with our creative spiritual intuition. This is how many new ideas are born.

Being in the zone on a regular basis can assist us in recognizing and strengthening our creative and intuitive gifts. Engaging a state of flow becomes easier and more natural as we seek more opportunities to use and expand our creative potential.

Being aware of the flow allows for more opportunities
to connect with your natural creative energy.

Flow is like boiling water. When you first set water to boil, there is minimal movement of molecules—the water is still. As you add heat, the water begins to increase its vibration and you start to see movement.

Tiny bubbles begin to appear and become larger and larger. Eventually, bubbles start to break the surface, and the water begins to boil. Add more heat and a low boil becomes a rapid boil. Now there's plenty of movement!

Being in the zone is much the same. At first, ideas float around in our heads but have little energy. As we focus on a specific subject, we begin to add "heat" in the form of our focus. Focus, like heat, increases vibration. As we continue to focus, our ideas start to branch off other ideas, and eventually the biggest ideas bubble to the surface. Suddenly we are boiling with energy and creativity. We are now in the flow.

When are you most in the flow?

How could being in the zone possibly help you bring about change in your current situation?

I know that I am a creative being and that creative energy is always flowing to me and through me.

Awareness Exercise #1: Brain Drain

This exercise can be used anytime you start feeling overwhelmed by too many thoughts or feelings.

Begin by taking out a piece of paper and pen (or start an electronic page), and set an alarm for fifteen minutes. Write down everything that is currently going on in your mind. You can write about anything from the "things I'm going to complete today" to the dreams you had last night—whatever is on your mind. When fifteen minutes are over, stop writing. Take notice of how you feel. Relieved? Less stressed?

The goal of this exercise is to *drain your brain* of the chatter that prevents you from sifting through your thoughts and feelings. The act of writing allows us to release energy onto the page instead of allowing our swirling thoughts and feelings to occupy the valuable space we need to think and stay focused.

You can try using *Brain Drain* first thing in the morning—it can help to "clear your palate" for the day. If you want to make some serious progress, try *Brain Drain* each morning for a week. Notice if your ability to focus improves. With new space released, new creative ideas can begin bubbling to the surface.

Awareness Exercise #2: Whose Voice Is That Anyway?

Thoughts, feelings, and intuition can each be given a voice (words that we hear inside our heads). When we say things like, "Let me tell you what I'm thinking," "My gut feeling is telling me this isn't a good idea," or "I don't believe that," we are activating a natural connection to our internal voices. There is a catch, however. Many of our internal messages are not coming from our own experiences—they are coming from the words of others.

So how do we know which voices are helpful and which are not? Start by asking questions.

When you initiate the exercise *Whose Voice Is That Anyway?*, you embark on an investigation to find the original source of a thought or belief. The next time you encounter a thought that your intuition tells you just doesn't "feel right," stop and ask yourself, "Where did that belief come from? How did I arrive at that opinion? Who said that to me?" You may quickly realize you are repeating something that someone else told you was true. Asking these questions lets you identify the voice of a teacher, parent, or friend who gave you advice. Even though you may have trusted that person, the information was coming to you from *their* experience, not yours.

The next question is, "Is this true for *me*?" If the belief does, in fact, serve you, then continue to use it. If not, think again—activate your power of choice and choose a new thought. Eventually that new thought will become your new belief.

Chapter 2: Moving Into Alignment

*If you are attuned to your inner guidance,
there is no way you can become severely out
of balance with your natural environment.*
Shakti Gawain

Moving into alignment is the second step to finding better balance. Alignment happens both on the inside and outside of us. Alignment means that our thoughts, beliefs, and intentions are aligned with our deepest truth and best understanding of our purpose in the world. Internally, this means that we strive to be conscious of our thoughts, feelings, and intuition so that our behaviors reflect our true values. Externally, this means that over time, we bring our attitudes, actions, and words closer and closer to our fundamental beliefs.

The next seven days will be spent taking a closer look at alignment. Focusing on alignment helps us reconnect with our natural state of balance and reminds us that the power to change our lives is always in our hands.

Day 8: The Body

> *Your body is a temple, but*
> *only if you treat it as one.*
> Astrid Alauda

The body is our shell and the home for our mind and spirit. The body is an elaborate and complex machine that also serves as a signaling device. Our body always tells us what it wants and needs—the question is whether we are listening. Physical health is an indicator of healthy body balance, but pain, illness, and disease are signals telling us to pay attention to our bodies.

Keeping the body in healthy balance is largely contingent upon three primary factors: diet, exercise, and the reduction of stress. Foods rich in protein, vitamins, and minerals along with complex carbohydrates provide the body with proper nutrition to maintain muscle and bone health. Adequate amounts of water keep the body hydrated and functioning at its optimum. Regular exercise is an essential ingredient to physical health and well-being. Developing a healthy routine of engaging in physical exercise and activities that calm and relax the body on a regular basis can significantly reduce stress.

The body can best support the mind and spirit when it is communicating effectively with them. Maintaining a consistent alignment of our thoughts, feelings, and intuition helps to keep our energies balanced and contributes to our physical health.

Alignment with your body supports physical, intellectual, emotional, and spiritual well-being.

The body is like a car. Cars come in different shapes and sizes, colors, makes, and models. But all cars have three things in common: They are unique, they require fuel, and each needs a driver.

Keeping a car running smoothly and in alignment requires regular maintenance including oil changes, fluid checks, and replacing parts when necessary. Regular cleaning helps reduce rust and keeps the body strong.

Like a car, the human body comes in assorted shapes, sizes, and colors. Our bodies require fuel in the form of food and drink, and each of us has a driver in charge of operation and maintenance. A body that is neglected will not operate efficiently. We can care for our body by fueling it with foods that support strength and good health; we can schedule regular check-ups for health and wellness; and we can choose to keep our bodies clean, fit, and strong.

Has your physical health been affected by your current situation? If so, in what ways?

How could listening to your body help you find better body balance?

I commit to loving my body. As I take care of my body and listen to its messages, I will be guided to better health, strength, and balance.

Day 9: Relationships

Alignment

> *Our greatest joy and our greatest pain*
> *come in our relationships with others.*
> Stephen R. Covey

Relationships are an essential part of life and help us to define who we are. We are naturally wired to connect and collaborate with others—those with the same energy source contained within ourselves—the collective human life force. This is why relationships are so powerful.

Relationships help us to create our unique life experience. When we enter into any relationship—regardless of whether it is with a co-worker, family member, friend, or romantic partner—we agree to exchange energy to assist one another in the process of creating ourselves. Without relationships, we would have little or no contrast, and without contrast we would not experience our being. Relationships are entered into by choice. Balanced relationships are based in freedom, not obligation.

Healthy relationships are grounded in respect for oneself and respect for others. Our relationships are mirrors of our current relationship with ourselves. If we do not love and respect ourselves, we will lack the capacity to love and respect others. Through validation and feedback, our relationships reflect to us not only who we are, but also who we'd like to be. Throughout our lives, people become our role models and we become theirs. Whether we realize it or not, we are all leading by example.

Healthy alignment in your relationships will be reflected back to you as a deeper love and respect for yourself and others.

Relationships are like musical instruments. One instrument alone can play a solo. Adding another instrument allows the two to play in harmony.

Each new instrument added creates a deeper and larger sound. Continuing to add more and different instruments can eventually create an orchestra.

Relationships are similar. Alone, we are just one energy source. Add another person and we can create in harmony. Adding more people, like friends and family, will start to create a larger and deeper song. Eventually, we can create a symphony.

How are your relationships serving you? How are they holding you back? How are you serving others with your being?

What change could you make in your relationships to bring them into closer alignment with your purpose?

My relationships are balanced and healthy, and they complement my connections with others.

Day 10: Silence

> *We need silence to be able to touch souls.*
> Mother Theresa

When used regularly, silence is a powerful tool. The mind, body, and spirit are designed to be active and engaged, but they also require downtime for balance and refreshment. In moments of silence, we can reconnect with ourselves and gain insight, focus, and clarity. Silence can bring us into alignment with our thoughts and feelings and help us to hear the quiet spiritual voice of our intuition.

Taking time for silence is a critical step for moving into alignment. In silence, we can quiet our thoughts, acknowledge our emotions, and relax into our bodies. In other words, we calm our human *doing*. Whether we use meditation, prayer, or even just closing our eyes, moving into our inner silence allows us to reconnect with our spirit—our human *being*. In order to find silence, we may have to create space for solitude—simple, but not always easy.

Silence helps with problem solving and decision making. If we are unsure how to respond to a problem or situation, we can stop, find a quiet space within us, and ask for an answer. As we are waiting for answers, we can develop a calm demeanor, soften our stance, and practice patience. Often the answers to our most difficult questions lie within us. Silence reminds us to *begin within*.

Silence allows you to develop a deeper and more balanced connection with yourself.

Silence is like a spiritual retreat, a healing center, or a cabin in the woods—a place where we can go to be alone and reconnect with ourselves. While most traditional counseling is healing for the mind and physical therapy is healing for the body, silence is healing for the spirit.

We can create a space for silence by simply unplugging from the world and turning down the noise. TVs, radios, computers, and mobile phones are powerful means for connecting with others, but the point of silence is to connect with yourself. At first it may seem like you are missing out, but unplugging for periods of time will raise your frequency—and over time, can significantly strengthen and enrich your personal connections.

When we lower the volume on the *outside* of our lives, we raise the volume on the *inside*. In silence we can discover the true benefits of being still and listening to the calm rhythm within.

How are you using silence in your daily life? What do you experience as the benefits of silence? Where do you see the potential to expand your commitment to silence?

How can silence assist you with finding better balance in your current situation?

I am able to use silence as an active part of my life to help hear the quiet spiritual voice within me.

Day 11: Truth

Alignment

> *If you tell the truth, you don't*
> *have to remember anything.*
> Mark Twain

Truth is the heart of our integrity. Being true to ourselves and to our values is the essence of alignment. Our personal truth is rooted in the foundation of our belief systems, most of which were passed down to us by our parents, teachers, and others who "knew better." However, these mentors were only teaching what was true in their experience at that point in time. As we mature, we have the ability to reexamine our beliefs and challenge the validity of our truth. By examining new thoughts, we can create new beliefs.

We can discover our own truth by listening to our words and observing our own behaviors. We can experience the truth of others by becoming aware of their frequency, listening to their words, and looking into their eyes, which have been termed "the windows of the soul." Often, the truth speaks louder than words.

Living our truth takes courage. Choosing what we believe instead of what others think we should believe requires trust in ourselves. Living our truth demonstrates respect for ourselves; and in return, allowing others to live their truth shows respect for them. Respecting others honors their perspective. What may be true for one person may be far from the truth for another.

Being in alignment with your truth allows
you to live in transparency and authenticity.

Truth is like our skin. It's unique to each of us and visible to the rest of the world. We can adorn our skin, put tattoos or makeup on it, but its essence is still uniquely ours. We can hide it or show it, and that choice can change from day to day.

There are some parts of our skin we reveal only when we're intimate, and other parts we proudly display to everyone.

Similar to skin, our truth is unique to each of us and visible to the world. Just as we have different ways of showing our skin, we create new beliefs that we "wear" as our truth by expressing our thoughts and feelings. Depending on the circumstances, we can hide our truth or show it, and there are some parts of truth we reveal only to certain friends or loved ones.

How has truth, or lack of truth, played a role in your current situation?

In what ways can a shift in the way you approach truth help effect change in your situation?

I am aware of my truth, and I'm able to communicate it clearly with confidence.

Day 12: Intention

Alignment

> *Our lives are connected by a thousand*
> *invisible threads… our actions run as*
> *causes and return to us as results.*
> Herman Melville

Intention is the direct reflection of our deepest truth and belief systems. Finding the true heart of our intention starts by asking ourselves what we really want based on what we value. Sometimes this is the clearest when we are experiencing what we *don't* want! Contrasting our experiences helps us to create what we *do* want. In fact, some of our most powerful intentions are born in our moments of greatest contrast.

Intentions influence our thoughts and feelings. When we use contrast to decide what we want, we activate the power of our intention, and our thoughts and feelings initiate the process of creating. This action brings us back into alignment with our values.

Intention creates results. Whenever we "mention our intention," we proclaim our desires by sharing them with others. As our intentions become clearer, we begin to express them freely through our attitudes, actions, and words. The act of speaking our intentions aloud shifts them from wishful thinking into action. For every action— even an expressed thought or feeling—there is a reaction. Something always happens.

> **Aligning intention with your**
> **truth moves you into action.**

Intention is like an apple tree. The life of the tree begins by planting seeds. The seed is nourished by sunlight, rain, and earth. The seed will eventually grow into a tree that bears leaves, fruit, and more seeds. Through attention and nurturing, what started as a single seed creates more of itself.

Similarly, the sunlight of our thoughts, the waters of our feelings, and the deep earth of our creative energy nurture and cultivate our intentions as we physically, emotionally, and spiritually evolve. Eventually, the original seeds of our intentions will become the fruits of our speaking, acting, and being.

With time and patience we will create whatever we intend, even when it takes longer than expected to manifest. After all, an apple doesn't just instantly appear on the tree.

How does your intention support you in your current situation?

In what ways could you clarify and realign your intentions to effect change in your situation?

My intentions are clear and rooted in my truth.

Day 13: Purpose

> *When a great ship is in harbor and*
> *moored, it is safe, there can be no doubt.*
> *But that is not what great ships are built for.*
> Clarissa Pinkola Estés, Ph.D.

A sense of purpose—the feeling that we are here for a reason or have a role to fulfill—helps give our lives meaning and contributes to an overall sense of worthiness. Purpose is reflected in our actions when they are aligned with our truth, intentions, and belief systems—it is more about *who we are* than *what we do.*

Purpose is dynamic and changes according to the context in which we experience it. Feeling an internal sense of purpose can give us direction and help us with decision-making. Feeling an external sense of purpose can assist us with choosing how we demonstrate our gifts to the world—like our choice of job or career.

Feeling a sense of purpose brings us into alignment with our truth and intention.

When your purpose and truth are aligned,
you feel self-worth and trust in your direction.

Purpose is like a map or Global Positioning System (GPS). When planning a trip, we can use either a map or a GPS to choose our destination and the route to take us there. As we travel along our journey, the map or GPS keeps us aligned with our destination and reroutes us if we get off track. A map or GPS helps us to reach a destination.

Like a map or GPS, defining our purpose sets our direction. We take action based on our purpose, and the feedback from that experience tells us whether we are on the right track. We can examine every choice against our purpose and decide whether or not it helps us to get there. Redirecting our energies towards our purpose keeps us moving toward our goals.

When have you experienced a strong sense of purpose? What strengthened that experience? What weakened it?

What can you do to strengthen your sense of purpose?

I am aligned with my purpose.
It is reflected by what I am doing and
who I am being in each moment.

Day 14: Abundance

There are more things in heaven and earth, Horatio,
than are dreamt of in your philosophy.
William Shakespeare, Hamlet

Abundance is part of the natural flowing stream of well-being that is available to everyone at all times. We have access to this stream; but only if we believe and act as if we do. Abundance is not limited to physical things like money or possessions; abundance can come to us through loving relationships, joy, blessings, and peace of mind. This is how a person without many material possessions can feel "rich."

Access to abundance requires us to be in alignment. We can begin by sharing our time, talents, and treasures and by expressing our gratitude. Staying in alignment keeps us focused and connected with our intentions. The power of our focus activates the process of receiving, and feelings of abundance can begin to flow to us and through us.

If we truly desire something, we must ask for it. When we ask, our spirit responds and brings us those things that match our request. Receiving requires an understanding of how abundance is part of the answer to our desires.

Staying in alignment allows abundance to be
activated in the manifestation of your desires.

Abundance is like an aquifer—an underground layer of water-bearing rock. Below the surface of the earth are aquifers containing massive amounts of water from which groundwater is extracted. Unless we find a natural spring, we don't have access to this groundwater until we tap into it. Tapping latent ground water through a well releases the water and allows it to flow to the surface.

Like an aquifer, abundance is often below the surface and goes unnoticed until we tap into it. Being in alignment is the drill that releases the wellspring of abundance.

Once the well of abundance has been tapped, we can experience the benefits of being in alignment and can return to this ever-flowing source of well-being at all times.

How does your experience of abundance affect your choices every day?

What can you do to notice the abundance in your life on a regular basis?

I have access to abundance all times and in all situations. My life is abundant.

Alignment Exercise #1: Breathe Your Body

This exercise is designed to help you use breathing to benefit your physical, emotional, and spiritual health. It can be combined with any other exercise and used throughout the day in any environment and at any time.

Begin by making yourself comfortable. You can either sit or lie in a position that is most natural and relaxing for you. Close your eyes and focus on your breathing pattern. For the next minute, pay attention to the natural rhythm of your breath coming in and going out. Do not control it; just notice it.

Now take in a deep breath, hold it for two or three seconds, and then slowly exhale through your mouth. As you exhale, relax your shoulders and let them drop, soften your belly, and hold no tension. Breathe all of the air out. Take another deep breath and do the same thing. Take your time. Breathe one more time and exhale slowly. Breathe and relax.

With each subsequent breath, focus your thoughts and awareness on a single part of your body beginning with your head, moving down into your neck, shoulders, chest, and so on—each time focusing on bringing oxygen into that part of your body. Do this for each breath until you have *breathed* into your whole physical body. Each time you breathe and focus on a different body part, you draw attention to that area, and your attention includes energy that can help to relax and release any stress there.

After this exercise, take notice of your energy. Do you feel a deeper calm? Less stress? Besides the physical benefit of relaxation, focused breathing helps to oxygenate your system and allows you to literally *breathe your body* back into alignment.

Alignment Exercise #2: Find Your Center

This exercise is designed to help you focus your energy on the center of your body and keep your physical, emotional, and spiritual energies aligned. This exercise can be combined with your existing exercise program or integrated with *Breathe Your Body* or *Walking Meditation* (from Exercises for Activation following Chapter 3).

Begin by focusing your awareness on the center of your body as you perform your exercise or activity. As you bring your awareness to your body's center, imagine that your spine is a pillar and the source of your energy is coming from and returning to that pillar. This is your center. You can also imagine a colored light (white or yellow works well for healing) surrounding the pillar. As you breathe and focus on your center, imagine the light growing stronger and brighter. This visual will help to align and balance your energies.

As you continue to exercise, stretch, or breathe, keep bringing your awareness back to your center and notice how your body feels. Can you sense a feeling of balance? An increased feeling of alignment? A strong connection with your body? Try this exercise while engaging in any physical activity, or even when sitting still. Finding your center on a regular basis can help to bring feelings of grounding, strength, and better balance.

Chapter 3: The Key is Activation

The journey of 1,000 miles begins with a single step.
Lao-tzu

Awareness brings our attention to the critical factors affecting our balance; alignment helps focus our energy internally and externally; and activation puts theory into practice and ideas into motion. Without activation, good ideas are only ideas. Activation is the key to implementation and the third step to finding better balance.

The next seven days will be spent taking a closer look at activation. Focusing on activation helps us reconnect with our natural state of balance and reminds us that the power to change our lives is always in our hands.

Day 15: Choice

> *It is not our abilities that show*
> *who we truly are, it is our choices.*
> Albus Dumbledore,
> *Harry Potter* – J. K. Rowling

Choice is a wonderful gift. In choosing, we create our own unique experience. Each choice we make brings a different result, and our choices—like our experiences—are constantly changing. Choice is our most powerful tool.

Choices come from identifying what we want. Since we live in a world filled with contrast, it is often easier to recognize what we *don't* want rather than what we *do* want. This comparison helps us to validate our choices. With the increasing speed of technology and communication, many of us are overwhelmed, and as a result, we make hasty or impulsive choices. By reclaiming our freedom to choose, we regain our ability to make better choices.

We choose our response to our experiences. Feedback from our choices gives us the opportunity to make better or different choices in the future. Our attitude, perspective, and intentions are also choices. For example, we can choose to be disappointed by an unexpected result; alternatively, by practicing the act of allowing, we can learn to accept it. Understanding our power to choose gives us unlimited options—and if our current choices don't serve us, we can always *choose again*.

Activating choice lets you to reconnect
with the power of your truth and intention.

Choice is like going out for dinner. We choose the restaurant by location, atmosphere, and cuisine. After arriving, we pick our seating preference. Most entrees come with choices for side options, condiments, and food preparation.

We can make additional choices including special requests and beverages, or we can change our order completely. If we don't like the food or service, we may not choose that restaurant again. Our experiences teach us how to make better choices.

Similarly, life presents us with a wide variety of choices, and each choice brings us more options. Just like going out for dinner, life is a collection of different choices and outcomes. If we don't get the desired outcome, we can change our minds and choose again. Choices are abundant—there will always be more choices for us to make.

📖 How have your choices affected your current situation?

📖 In what ways can you choose something different?

**I am in control of my choices. I use
my power of choice to engage my mind,
body, and spirit to make healthy decisions.**

Day 16: Boundaries

Activation

> *We are drawn to each other because of our similarities,*
> *but it is our differences we must learn to respect.*
> Johann Wolfgang Von Goethe

Boundaries are the seen and unseen rules of engagement necessary for protection, safety, and respect. Personal boundaries are based in our truth, intention, and belief systems. Boundaries create a personal space within which we choose whom we allow access and how we want to be treated.

Our boundaries are dynamic and evolve over time. Our personal boundaries are often identified when they have been crossed or violated. In this way, contrast helps us to define and create new boundaries. Developing healthy personal boundaries is not a selfish act; it is an act of self-care. Communicating and reinforcing our personal boundaries shows respect for ourselves.

Equally as important is respecting other people's boundaries, especially when our views or opinions differ. Underdeveloped or "blurred" boundaries are evidenced by indecisiveness, aggressiveness, or a need to control others. If our goal is to have clear boundaries, we need to focus only on ourselves and learn to communicate our desires in healthy and respectful ways.

> ***Activating your boundaries creates***
> ***freedom and respect for yourself and others.***

Boundaries are like a home. A home has many different rooms—each room with its own unique purpose. Public spaces like an entryway, hallway, or living room tend to host a wide variety of people—friends, family, and sometimes strangers—and these boundaries are less restricted.

Other spaces like bedrooms, bathrooms, and personal offices are usually considered private. These personal spaces have deeper connections associated with them and are not usually entered without a host's permission.

Like a home, our boundaries define the energy spaces within us. People enter into our lives in both public and personal ways through relationships at work, personal friends, family, and intimate partners. Like the rooms of a house, each relationship has different boundaries according to the nature of the relationship. If we choose, we can let people enter different areas our lives by opening the doors when we feel trust and mutual respect for one another.

How have you established your personal boundaries? Where do your boundaries need rethinking?

How could adjusting your boundaries help effect change in your current situation?

I have healthy personal boundaries. I am able to communicate them clearly and easily to others.

Day 17: Perspective

> *You are the window through
> which you see the world.*
> George Bernard Shaw

Perspective is our current viewpoint or frame of reference. Perspective comes to us from our perceptions about the present and the past. Our perspective is strongly based in our truth and is greatly influenced by our thoughts and feelings. We form our perspective based on our beliefs, past experiences, and current conditions.

Our perspective can be chosen. We can change our attitude by reframing or looking at a situation from a different perspective. We can choose to be either optimistic and focus on the positive aspects of any situation, or pessimistic and focus on the negative. By reframing an event with a perspective of gratitude instead of disappointment, a situation originally perceived as negative can become positive. Reframing supports our power to choose again.

The act of introspection allows us to gain better perspective on ourselves. We can find introspection by engaging in silence or through other activities like traveling or simply drinking iced tea on a hot summer's day. Engaging in introspection can help us learn to appreciate our talents and achievements. Equally as important is learning to honor and respect the perspectives of others. Each of us can receive a different message from the same story.

*Activating your perspective allows you
to see things from multiple views and
respond in healthy and balanced ways.*

Perspective is like altitude. If you were standing on a train station platform and asked to count the individual train cars as a train was speeding by, it may be impossible.

However, if you were in an airplane or helicopter above the same train, you would see it from a different perspective. The higher you rose, the slower the train would appear to be moving and the easier it would be to count the number of individual cars.

Similarly, our "altitude" greatly influences our perspective of what we are able to see or understand about a given situation. In the midst of the action, our perspective about something can feel frustrating or overwhelming. From where we are standing, the events may be rushing by so quickly that we are unable to see them for what they are. If we are able to "rise above it," we can get a higher perspective and reframe our viewpoint to the larger picture.

How has your perspective contributed to your current situation?

How could you change your perspective?

I am able to choose and reframe my perspective to one that serves me.

Day 18: Focus

*The shorter way to do many things
is to do only one thing at a time.*
Wolfgang Amadeus Mozart

Focus is an essential part of the creative process. Focus involves concentration, which comes when we have fewer distractions. The world is overflowing with more distractions each day, but we have the ability to limit our distractions by using our power of choice. With practice and attention, we can learn to harness and control our focus.

Focus can lead us into or out of balance quickly. By raising our awareness, we may find that we are giving too much of our attention to unhealthy habits or to people who don't serve us. With this knowledge, we have the ability to gently shift our focus back to ourselves and choose activities and relationships that are in alignment with our goals and intentions.

Focus requires prioritization. In a busy world, we may often find it challenging to focus our attention. Since our minds have difficulty concentrating on more than one thing at a time, prioritizing what we focus on becomes increasingly important. Refining our ability to find and maintain our focus will allow more of our energy to flow towards the most important thing at any moment. Focus can increase our flow of creative energy and help us to tap more of our potential.

***Activating your focus allows you to organize,
prioritize, and move into greater creative flow.***

Focus is like RAM (random access memory) in a computer. The more programs that are running simultaneously, the less efficiently RAM operates. Eventually the computer's performance becomes sluggish, or in a worst-case scenario, it crashes. Similarly, the more ideas, tasks, and responsibilities we are thinking about, the less capacity we have to stay focused. Our brain can also overload and, like the computer, "crash."

Creating space allows for better focus. Releasing more memory space in our minds is like freeing up RAM on our computer. Just like closing computer programs, we reduce clutter by expressing our thoughts and feelings through speaking or writing. Activities such as journaling, making lists, and jotting notes throughout the day are great ways to make more space for new thoughts, increase our creative capacity, and help us to maintain our focus. (See *Brain Drain* in Exercises for Awareness).

Where have you been putting your focus? How is that serving you? How is it getting in your way?

How would it affect your current situation to shift your focus?

I am able to establish and maintain my focus and move into greater creative flow.

Day 19: Empathy

> *My life is my message.*
> Mahatma Ghandi

Empathy is a form of sympathy with a healthy and balanced perspective. Whereas sympathy says, "I feel your pain and I am with you," empathy says, "I can imagine how you must feel and I support you." Empathy recognizes the connection that exists between all human beings. Empathy involves reaching out in love and respect for others while maintaining healthy balance for ourselves.

Displaying empathy doesn't include rescuing others from their feelings or the consequences of their choices. Empathy is respectful and allows everyone to take responsibility for their own experience. Respecting ourselves means providing support for others without losing the integrity of our own boundaries in the process.

Showing empathy and providing support for others is most effective when we are healthy and supported ourselves. When we are well-balanced, we are better able to listen, comfort, and support others. Being self-supportive requires a dedication to self-care, wellness, and a commitment to healing our own unresolved issues and pain. Caring for others in a healthy way means caring for ourselves first.

Activating empathy allows you to give support in healthy and balanced ways.

Empathy is like a lighthouse. A lighthouse is most effective when it is functioning at its best—its lens is clean and clear, its light is shining brightly, and its structure is standing sturdy and stalwart. When a lighthouse is functioning well, it is a beacon guiding ships to shore during fog or the dark of night. It is reliable and consistent because it has been cared for and maintained.

When we practice empathy, we are like the lighthouse. We can provide support to others by acting as a beacon to help guide them when they need it, but we cannot rescue them. Our job is not to save others, it is to support others—we cannot be both the lighthouse and the Coast Guard. Empathy lets us stay strong and grounded while allowing others to step into their own strength and courage.

Where are you demonstrating empathy in your life? Where do you desire to demonstrate more empathy?

How can empathy help you move forward?

I am able to express empathy and be supportive of others while maintaining support for myself.

Day 20: Allowing

> *"For I know the plans I have for you," declares*
> *the Lord, "plans to prosper you and not to harm*
> *you, plans to give you hope and a future."*
> The Bible, Jeremiah 29:11

Allowing is accepting the present moment. The present is the only moment we can fully and completely experience in our physical dimension. Our thoughts and feelings can take us into past memories or imagine future events, but our physical bodies exist only in the present.

Allowing requires patience and understanding. Developing a higher tolerance for ambiguity lets us be present and curious at the same time. With the power of positive thinking, doubt can shift into anticipation. Saying, "I don't know what's going to happen next... and that excites me," opens us up to welcoming the unexpected. Allowing lets us believe, "If not this, something better."

Allowing releases control and honors the process of becoming. It reminds us that our life "is what it is," and that we can let go of the need to micromanage every piece of it. Allowing teaches us to accept all things, including people, *as they are*. Even when we have the responsibility to support someone as a parent, boss, or teacher, we cannot assume responsibility for the consequences of their decisions. Allowing lets us support and guide others in a healthy and balanced way.

Allowing activates a healthy acceptance of yourself and others.

Allowing is like exhaling. Breathing is something we do both consciously and unconsciously. Conscious breathing brings awareness to how we use our breath proactively. When we hold our breath—which we often associate with something that's either exciting or fearful—we experience a feeling of being in control.

Conscious exhaling creates feelings of release. When panicked or stressed, we may hear a friend tell us to "stop and breathe." The act of exhaling allows us to expand, relax, and release.

Allowing lets us exhale and release the need to control everything and everyone in our lives—we can learn how to *truly let go*. Like exhaling, allowing brings relief. When we learn to allow things and people to be as they are, we experience the freedom to stay focused on ourselves and allow others to do the same.

What are you allowing in your current situation? Where are you unable to let go?

How could allowing help you?

I am allowing people and circumstances around me to be as they are while I maintain my focus.

Day 21: Gratitude

> *As we express our gratitude, we must*
> *never forget that the highest appreciation*
> *is not to utter words, but to live by them.*
> John F. Kennedy

Gratitude is the act of appreciation that comes from our spirit and manifests itself through our feelings. Gratitude is a state of being—a humble, thankful response to something we've just received or to something we already have. Developing an attitude of gratitude keeps us in alignment with our truth and intentions, while feelings of gratitude contribute to our physical and emotional well-being.

We often think of gratitude as spontaneous, but we can practice gratitude. Since thankfulness is rooted in positive feelings, feeling and expressing gratitude creates more positive energy. Being thankful generates a spirit of genuine appreciation, and feelings of goodwill always inspire more of the same. Appreciating ourselves and celebrating our gifts and talents can also express gratitude.

Gratitude completes the loop in the giving and receiving cycle. When we give something to someone and they express to us their gratitude, it confirms and validates our intentions. Gratitude becomes an opportunity to create deeper connections with others and develop an authentic appreciation for them.

Activating gratitude allows you to recognize and express genuine appreciation for yourself and others.

Gratitude is like a "thank you" card—a gift *back* for a gift given. When we take time to show our appreciation for someone's gift, we make an exchange of spiritual energy.

Gratitude allows for this spiritual connection to occur. This exchange adds to the foundation of our relationship and strengthens the bonds of trust and respect. Expressions of gratitude are seldom forgotten.

Just like a thank you card, we can give ourselves gratitude by writing down appreciation we've received from others. By starting a list entitled *Nice Things People Have Said About Me,* we can remember the compliments and gratitude we've received from others. Remembering kind words of appreciation can bring us the same feelings of gratitude years later when we reread our list again.

How are you currently practicing gratitude? What are you most thankful for? Are you taking time to express gratitude to others?

How could you sharpen your powers of appreciation and thankfulness? How might that change your current situation?

I am able to express my gratitude freely and easily for all that I have and all that I receive.

Book Two

21 Steps to Better Relationships

Find More Balance with Others

Introduction

Relationships are the foundation of our personal growth and expansion in this lifetime. We are naturally wired to connect and collaborate with others—those with the same energy source contained within ourselves—the collective human life force. Regardless of whether the relationship is with a family member, significant other, co-worker, friend, or acquaintance, all of our relationships are extremely powerful and assist us in creating our life stories.

Balanced relationships contain core essential elements including respect, appreciation, and freedom. In a balanced relationship, each person is responsible for his or her own behavior. Balanced relationships are equitable; both people contribute equally. Lack of balance in a relationship can show up as criticism, control, or neglect. Unhealthy relationships not only erode the mind and body, they create barriers and slow our spiritual growth.

Remember: The power to change your relationships is *always* in your hands. Make a commitment to pay closer attention to your interactions with others and create the momentum to bring more love, peace, joy, and harmony to all of your relationships. It's your choice.

Chapter 4: Welcome to Awareness

*I awoke, only to find that the rest
of the world is still asleep.*
Leonardo da Vinci

Our relationships are central to understanding our purpose in this lifetime. We learn from our connections with others through our similarities and contrasts. We make choices by harnessing the power of our thoughts, feelings, and intuition. In order to find better balance with others, we must first become aware of the factors that influence our relationships.

The first seven steps focus on awareness. Raising our awareness reminds us that the power to change our relationships always begins with noticing what's happening in the present moment.

Step 1: Know Thyself

This above all: to thine own self be true,
And it must follow, as the night the day,
Thou canst not then be false to any man.
William Shakespeare

All relationships begin with you. The words "Know Thyself" were inscribed on the entrance to the Temple of Apollo at Delphi thousands of years ago. Knowing your current limitations and learning from your experience continue to be essential today. Take the time to develop the most important relationship—the one with yourself.

To know yourself is to love and accept yourself *as you are*—even with the attributes you strive to improve. Being in a healthy relationship with yourself starts with the awareness of your thoughts, feelings, and intuition, and then using that knowledge in your life and relationships. Your experiences become your story. Only *you* are the expert on your life.

Relationships with others are always a direct reflection of the relationship you have with yourself. When you know yourself—your strengths, joys, limitations, and fears—you can present yourself to others with truth and transparency. Take the time to know yourself—your *best* self. Know that you have worth and value. Believe in yourself and others will believe in you.

Being aware of who you are brings truth and transparency to your relationships.

It was apparent at an early age that I was gifted with an abundance of energy, naturally extroverted, and happiest around people. It wasn't until after college, when I moved to Hawaii, that I started exploring my true *expanded* self. I found balance for my exuberance by connecting with the quiet spirit within—a deeply curious side of me that was hungry for more meaning.

As I began to spend more time with myself, I learned to appreciate the value of solitude. I had always been energized by people, but I was now also energized by nature. I had discovered a newfound peace in simply watching waves and appreciating sunsets.

This new relationship with myself was exhilarating! Once I became acquainted with my deeper inner self, I was able to stretch my imagination to new heights. I found myself with access to a wider variety of thoughts, emotions, and creative energies than ever before.

In what ways could you know yourself better? What parts of yourself seem undeveloped, hidden, or mysterious?

In what ways do your closest relationships help you to be your "best self"?

Excuse Me, Who Are You?

Make a list of the most important people in your life, and then answer the following questions: How do those who love you see you differently? What feels true? What feels false or inauthentic? Which relationships reflect your best self, and which reflect the parts you want to change? Recognize and appreciate your ability to become aware of your relationships and how they are reflections of you.

Step 2: Communication

> *First learn the meaning of*
> *what you say, then speak.*
> Epictetus

Through communication, we interact with others, sharing beliefs, values, and intentions. Words, though powerful, are only a small part of giving and receiving information. We also communicate through tone, expressions, and body language. Open, effective, two-way communication is the cornerstone of all healthy balanced relationships. Effective communication in relationships is founded on honesty and truth.

In order to communicate in healthy and balanced ways, we must pay attention to how we are feeling as we are sending or receiving information. Becoming aware of our emotions helps us to communicate and sort through our thoughts and feelings, especially when our emotions have been triggered. Even though our human nature is to be reactive, we can have full control over how we *respond* to the world around us. By acknowledging our feelings and thinking carefully before we speak, we can choose our words wisely and respond to others clearly and calmly.

Awareness of effective communication is
vital for creating healthy relationships.

Donna and Kevin have been married for a year. The last time Kevin went out for a few beers with his friends, Donna blew up at him when he got home and angrily said that he's happy to go out with his friends, but he won't go out with her.

One evening last week, Kevin told Donna he needed to stay and work late. In reality, Kevin lied. Instead of working late, he was out with his friends again. Donna found out and was furious.

When Donna and Kevin sat down to talk about it, Kevin said that he was afraid to tell her that his time with friends is still very important to him. Donna said that she's happy that he is close to his friends, but that she thinks his time with his friends is cutting into the time they spend together. In the end, they decided to schedule a "date night" each week so they could go out with friends or on their own. They also agreed to make sure they were socializing as much with each other as they are separately. They found a peaceful compromise by communicating openly and honestly with each other.

What is communication like in your relationships? Where are you being less than honest or avoiding conflict? Where would you choose to be less forthcoming?

What would you like communication to be like? How could it work better?

Iceberg. Dead Ahead.

Pay attention to the next time your emotions are triggered during a conversation. What was said? What emotions were triggered? How can you avoid an emotional collision? Take a moment to pause, acknowledge your feelings, and think carefully about how to respond. Ask questions for clarification and be willing to investigate your feelings. Notice what's different when you come from a place of thoughtful response, and see how this changes the landscape of the conversation.

Step 3: Boundaries

> *How others treat me is their path;*
> *how I react is mine.*
> Dr. Wayne Dyer

Boundaries are the visible and invisible rules of engagement that we put in place for protection and safety. Boundaries create a personal space within which we are able to choose whom we allow access and how we want to be treated. Boundaries provide a framework for mutual understanding and respect for natural differences in all relationships.

Having healthy personal boundaries facilitates self-reliance and contributes to creating nurturing, productive, and respectful relationships with others. Having clear boundaries requires that we focus on ourselves and learn to communicate our desires in healthy and respectful ways. Setting our personal boundaries allows us to express our truth and beliefs to others with confidence and courage. Acknowledging others' boundaries demonstrates respect and builds trust.

Our relationships are the testing ground for healthy boundaries. Unhealthy boundaries are evidenced by indecisiveness, aggressiveness, and a need to control others. Balanced boundaries allow relationships where we care for ourselves without feeling the need to save or rescue others. Boundaries allow us to blend our energies with others and to co-create without losing ourselves in the process. One plus one still equals two.

Being aware of boundaries allows for
freedom and respect for yourself and others.

Shawn and I have been good friends for many years, and we have very similar amounts of creative energy. When we decided to become roommates, we thought living in the same apartment would be easy.

We understand each other well and have similar tastes. However, within the first week, we found ourselves on stimulus overload. We both realized that our highly energetic personalities also needed downtime. We needed to establish healthy boundaries.

Since we enjoyed spending time alone as much as we enjoyed spending time together, we came up with a plan to respect each other's need for solitude and focus. Whenever one of us was wearing ear buds, it meant we were "in the zone"—a time to be left alone. This simple visual cue let the other person know not to disturb us, and this healthy boundary helped to keep our relationship respectful and balanced.

What are your boundaries like in your current relationships?

Where do you need stronger boundaries to protect yourself? Where could your boundaries be more flexible?

Boundary Hunter

Think about a situation or a relationship when you were unclear about your personal boundaries. What happened? How did that lack of clarity affect your relationships? Now remember a time when you were very clear about your boundaries. What happened then? What do you notice about how your relationships were affected? What conclusions can you draw? Add these insights to your journal or write them down so you remember the importance of boundaries in the future.

Step 4: Frequency

Everyone is kneaded out of the same dough
but not baked in the same oven.
Yiddish proverb

Our "frequency" is our personal energetic level. Personal frequencies fluctuate between higher or lower levels depending on our present state of health, mood, or well-being. Similar to radio stations broadcasting different types of music, we feel a variety of energetic vibrations— or "vibes"—coming from other people. Being around someone who raises your frequency, or *lifts your mood*, feels much different than someone who *brings you down*.

Connect with your feelings and intuition to sense frequency. Our physical, emotional, and spiritual energy levels are influenced by our environment, and it's up to each of us to pay attention and maintain our own frequency. Sometimes this means disconnecting or detaching from others energetically for the purpose of self-preservation.

Frequency plays a critical role in relationships. Matching frequencies in the workplace can be challenging, as our ability to choose our relationships is more limited. Our personal relationships offer us more freedom of choice. The interplay of frequency in relationship is often overlooked but worth paying attention to. The frequencies of the people around us can reinforce our own, or they can act as a counter-balance. Either can be beneficial depending on the situation. Awareness is key.

Being aware of your frequency allows
you to notice how relationships affect you.

Serena recently moved to a new team within her organization. In her previous role, Serena got along with her other team members but didn't feel closely connected to them. Her job was fine, but she wasn't passionate or excited about it.

During the first week in her new role, Serena noticed her frequency shifting. Her new team felt different. One team member, Tom, had new and exciting perspectives, and was always sharing them with Serena and the team. Working with Tom increased Serena's energy level and improved her productivity. Her increased productivity boosted Serena's confidence, which gave her courage to share her ideas more openly and freely.

What do you notice about the frequencies of the people you're closest to? Do you see any commonalities?

What do you know about your personal frequency? When do you need counter-balancing from others? When is contrast good for you?

The Good, The Bad, and The Ugly

Given what you know about the frequencies of your key relationships, what actions can you take this week to be in better balance with others? Whom do you need to spend more time with? Whom might you need to disconnect or protect yourself from? Take a moment and jot down these changes in your calendar or to-do list for the coming week.

Step 5: Love

Awareness

> *And all I'm saying is, see, what a wonderful*
> *world it would be if only we'd give it a chance.*
> *Love, baby, love. That's the secret, yeah.*
> Louis Armstrong

Love comes from reconnection to the flow of well-being that is a natural and abundant part of our lives. Love is the connection to God, Source Energy, The Universe—the life force of which we are all made. Love is the spiritual glue that binds us together. It may be difficult to explain what love is, but we know how love feels.

Our relationships with others are the manifestation of the love we have inside reflected back to us through the eyes and hearts of others. When our hearts are filled with love for ourselves, we have a larger capacity to feel and experience love for others. Loving and being loved increase and heighten our sense of well-being—when we love, we are less resistant and open to more of the positive energy that is flowing to and through us.

Relationships with those who *know your heart* create opportunities for mutual expansion. When someone says "I love you," they are putting their faith in you and the potential for a deeper connection is created. This kind of love is truth-telling and unconditional—it respects someone for their strengths while acknowledging their shortcomings.

Awareness of love within us and in our
relationships helps us reconnect with ourselves.

While reading a book and sharing special time with her father, 3-year-old Alyssa stopped, looked up, and said, "Daddy, I love you so much." The feeling of love was so real in Alyssa that she just said it out loud. Children are very skilled at expressing their joy in the moment. Perhaps we can take some lessons from the children in our lives and remember how to express love more freely and openly.

📖 In what ways does love flow through your closest relationships?

📖 What would it take for you to spend more time being in a state of loving and being loved by others or to reconnect with your divine source of love?

✋ **Love Break**

When do you feel most fully loved and loving? Take a moment to make a list of the times in your life when positive loving energy flows through you. Then look at your calendar for the next three weeks and plan at least one "love break" per week. Some examples may include: cuddling with your dog or cat, a date night with your sweetheart, climbing a nearby mountain, spending an evening with a close friend, or attending a session of meditation or prayer.

Step 6: Power

Awareness

> *I hope our wisdom will grow with our power,*
> *and teach us that the less we use our power,*
> *the greater it will be.*
> Thomas Jefferson

Power is the possession of authority, control, or influence over others. People demonstrate power through attitudes, actions, and words. Power can be used consciously or unconsciously, to manipulate and abuse or to support and encourage.

People can feel powerful or powerless depending on their circumstances. By understanding power, and using it effectively, we can dramatically affect our relationships.

Creating an equitable and healthy balance of power is key in balanced relationships. In relationships, individual power must be respected. Relationships provide the means for using personal power while still remaining open and receptive to the power of others. Engaging in power struggles only results in anger, frustration, and disappointment. We can release the need to control by reminding others of their power, or *empowering* them.

Becoming aware of your power helps you to create more balanced relationships.

John's boss was out of touch with her power. Andrea was well-educated, socially savvy, and professionally astute, but she had fought for so many years to get to the top that she couldn't turn off her aggressiveness. Since she wasn't aware of how to use and diffuse her power, Andrea micromanaged many of John's activities, leaving him feeling frustrated and powerless.

Finally, John learned how to regain his power in the relationship. His awareness that Andrea was out of touch with her power gave him the ability to work smarter. Even though he didn't agree with all of Andrea's ideas, he started to work *with her* out of compassion instead of *against her* out of anger.

John found that if he didn't push against Andrea, he could gradually introduce ideas that would complement rather than challenge her. Over time, they were both able to achieve the results they wanted and John no longer felt overpowered.

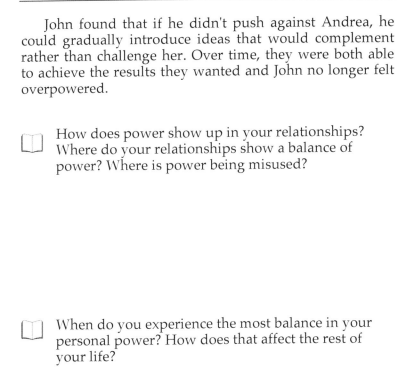

How does power show up in your relationships? Where do your relationships show a balance of power? Where is power being misused?

When do you experience the most balance in your personal power? How does that affect the rest of your life?

Power Trip

Think of people in your life who are very powerful. What makes them appear powerful? Now think of people you'd consider power hungry or out of touch with their power. What makes them seem that way? Spend a week noticing how you and the people around you use power. How does power affect your relationships with others every day?

Step 7: Freedom

> *Liberation isn't about breaking out of anything;*
> *it's a gentle melting into who we really are.*
> Marianne Williamson

Freedom is a basic human need. As powerful as love and as desired as trust, freedom comes when control and expectations are released. We tend to want to control our immediate environment, including the people in it—but learning to release the need to control is the key to finding better balance in any relationship. Balanced relationships are always based in freedom, not obligation.

The amount of freedom in our relationships often reflects the personal freedom we have experienced in our own lives. Freedom for ourselves includes taking responsibility to heal our pain, resolve our conflicts, and create healthy boundaries. Once we've learned to love and accept ourselves, the door is open to love and accept others.

Freedom in relationships is an essential component for creating harmony and balance. When people are personally responsible for their choices and behaviors, they will experience freedom in action.

Understanding your personal freedom will bring more freedom to your relationships.

Chris and Brian had been dating for nearly two years. Whenever the subject of marriage came up, Brian would say very little or change the subject. One evening, as they were watching a TV program about backpackers trekking through Europe, Chris noticed Brian's eyes widen with curiosity. Brian told Chris he'd always dreamed of backpacking through Europe for six months. Chris asked if this was still his dream, and Brian said yes—at least he thought so.

And then Brian realized why he'd been avoiding the marriage conversation—he assumed that if they got married, his travel dream would never come true.

Chris assured Brian that if his travel dream was so important, he should do it—even after they were married. After knowing that he was still free to continue making his own choice, Brian realized he really wasn't interested in traveling with a backpack for six months anymore—it had sounded much better when he was in college. His dream of travel had evolved. In fact, maybe now they could travel to Europe together for a week-long honeymoon instead.

How is freedom showing up in your connections with other people?

When do you feel most free? When are you able to offer the most freedom in your relationships? Notice how the answers to those questions are related.

Free to Be, You and Me

This week, take a freedom inventory in your current relationships. Answer the questions above and think about how you are free, and allowing others to be free, in your relationships. Where are you holding on where you could let go? When do you feel most "free to be?" What can you do this week to move toward greater freedom for yourself or for someone you love?

Exercise for Awareness: This is Your Life

This exercise is meant to be done alone. It is designed to help you become aware of the people and relationships which have had a positive influence on you.

First, think of a person who has shared with you either wise words, helpful advice, or a guiding hand. This person may be a teacher, coach, friend, or parent—someone whose words or actions have made a lasting impression on you. This person may be from your Call to Action list in Step 1.

Next, write down their name and what you received from them. For example, in my life I was uplifted and encouraged by my high school music teacher, Mrs. Bradley. Mrs. Bradley believed in me and my talents, taught me to express my creative and musical self with confidence, and allowed me the opportunity to let my light shine for others to see. Her unfailing encouragement and support made such a powerful impact on my self-esteem that I feel the benefit of her guidance to this day.

Repeat this exercise with each person who has made a significant impression on your life path, and notice how it reinvigorates your sense of appreciation and gratitude.

Now choose at least one of the people on your list and get in touch with them somehow. You can write them a letter, send an email, call them on the phone—whatever it takes—and tell them specifically how they've affected your life. They will certainly appreciate the kindness, and you will feel fantastic! Expressions of gratitude are seldom forgotten.

Chapter 5: Moving Into Alignment

Your task is not to seek for love,
but merely to seek and find all of the
barriers within yourself that
you have built against it.
Rumi

Moving into alignment is the second stage to finding better balance in relationships. Alignment happens when we connect with our deepest values, goals, and life purpose, and it is evidenced both inside and outside of us. As we move in and out of alignment with our deepest selves, our relationships directly reflect our present state of balance. The alignment process in relationships is always changing and can be influenced and understood through the awareness of our thoughts, feelings, and intuition.

The next seven steps will be spent taking a closer look at alignment. Focusing on alignment connects us with our deepest purpose, brings us into better balance with ourselves, and reminds us that knowing what we truly want helps us to create the relationships we desire most.

Step 8: Trust *Alignment*

> *Ask yourself if you would feel comfortable*
> *giving your two best friends a key to your house.*
> *If not, look for some new best friends.*
> H. Jackson Brown, Jr.

Trust, the foundation for all healthy and balanced relationships, is believing in someone's reliability, integrity, competence, or strength. In close personal relationships, trust means believing that someone is essentially on your side and that differences are not fundamental barriers to your connection. Trust creates and maintains connections between people.

Trust begins with you. Trust is grounded in your personal integrity and in your empathy for other people. When you know yourself, you know your truths and beliefs. When you trust yourself, you give others the opportunity to trust you. Integrity, truth, honesty, and transparency build trust. Kindness, compassion, and a spirit of genuine connection maintain trust and create authenticity and respect.

Trust is often referred to as *earned* since it is created over time and consciously maintained. When someone says, "I trust you," they are putting their faith in you, and a mutual connection is created. This connection is to be taken seriously. If trust is lost—either with others or yourself—it can be restored through forgiveness and grace.

Developing and trusting yourself
brings trust into your relationships.

When Jimmy was three years old, he was out in a boat in the middle of the lake with his dad and Uncle Frank. When they asked him if he'd like to go in the water, Jimmy said no at first. "Don't worry," Uncle Frank said, "I'll be holding you the entire time. You will love it! Trust me."

After a bit of coaxing, Jimmy's dad put a life jacket on him and lowered him into the water and his uncle's waiting arms. From that point on, swimming in the middle of the lake became a tradition for Jimmy every summer.

When Jimmy's daughter, Nicki, was three years old, they were visiting Grandpa's cabin and took the boat out for an afternoon cruise. When they got to the middle of the lake, Jimmy asked Nicki if she'd like to go in the water. "Don't worry," Jimmy said, "I'll be holding you the entire time. You will love it! Trust me." After a bit of coaxing, Nicki finally let Grandpa put a life jacket on her and lower her into her dad's arms. From that point on, swimming in the middle of the lake became a tradition for Nicki every summer.

What is necessary for you to feel trust in a person or a relationship?

Where do you trust yourself, and where do you feel mistrustful or out of alignment with your own intentions?

In We I Trust

Take a moment to think of the closest people in your life whom you trust and who trust you. What is the nature of your relationship? How has that trust been earned? What did it take? What can you do to earn other people's trust? What will it take? Notice this week when you are relying on someone's trust or they're relying on yours and appreciate the value of your trusting relationships.

Step 9: Intention
Alignment

> *What you are now choosing to believe and think and say*
> *will create the next moment and the next day*
> *and the next month and the next year.*
> Louise Hay

Intention is the direct reflection of our deepest truth and belief systems. Our intentions form the foundation for our attitudes, actions, and words. Intentions move from thought into word, word into action, and action into being.

Intention in relationships begins with identifying what we want. Our desires are fueled by our beliefs, goals, and the experiences of our previous relationships. Even knowing what we *don't* want gives us information and the opportunity to create what we *do* want. Once our intentions are known, they must still be re-evaluated over time. Even the best intentions can create unexpected or undesired results.

When your behavior is in alignment with your intentions, it is easier to evaluate the intentions and expectations of others. When you clearly discuss your intentions, you plant seeds for collaboration and co-creation. Balance in relationships can be maintained as long as intentions are continually clarified and mutually understood. Nobody wants to be left out of the loop.

> ***Keeping your intentions and actions in***
> ***alignment helps to balance relationships.***

Scott was hired for a new job as a program manager, responsible for realigning the customer service department in a struggling business. Known for being creative and innovative, Scott was very excited to bring his expertise to this new role. He was also really happy to find a job in tough economic times after looking for more than a year.

After two weeks on the job, Scott presented his goals for the realignment: to improve quality and service by developing a new training program. Although his boss, Sanjeev, agreed that training was important, he challenged Scott's position.

Scott's focus was to improve the customer experience with more training; Sanjeev's focus was to make more money, not spend it. As Scott continued to support his position, Sanjeev became more frustrated. Unfortunately, the meeting ended poorly. Within a week, Scott left the company. As he began interviewing for his next job, Scott put together a list of questions that focused on the hiring manager's intentions for the company and the position. He resolved to make sure that his intentions matched the company's before he got on-board.

How are your actions aligned with your intentions in your relationships?

What do you know about the intentions of the people you're closest to? Where are you matched up? Where are you out of alignment with each other?

I'll take Joy for 500, Alex.

Think of a time where your intentions were clear and results were a perfect match. How did your intentions keep you focused? Now think of a time when your intentions were very different from the result. What was missing? What did you learn? Write down these examples and keep them for future reference. There is value in learning from your own experiences.

Step 10: Purpose

> *We don't set out to save the world;*
> *we set out to wonder how other people*
> *are doing and to reflect on how our*
> *actions affect other people's hearts.*
> Pema Chodron

A sense of purpose—the feeling that we are here for a reason or have a role to fulfill—helps give our lives meaning and contributes to an overall sense of worth. When we enter into any relationship, we agree to assist one another in the creative process. Whether the relationship includes physical, emotional, intellectual, or spiritual exchange, the foundation of every relationship is to fulfill a need and create an experience that would be impossible alone.

Purpose can be an indicator and give us direction. Our lives provide us with a revolving door of people moving in and out—friends, co-workers, roommates, romantic partners, family members, and sometimes even strangers—who assist us, teach us, or bring contrast to help us define our own purpose more clearly. At the same time, our relationships with them reveal their purposes just as clearly. Relationships help us each clarify the vision, form our intentions, and collaborate to take action. The strongest relationships help us understand and celebrate our differences.

Balanced relationships help us stay true
to our purpose individually and together.

There is a story about an old woman who had two large pots for carrying water, each hung on the ends of a pole that she carried across her neck. One of the pots had a crack in it while the other pot was perfect. At the end of the long walks from the stream to the house, the cracked pot arrived only half full.

After two years of what it perceived to be bitter failure, the cracked pot spoke to the woman one day. "I'm ashamed of myself, because this crack in my side causes water to leak out all the way back to your house." The old woman smiled and replied, "Did you notice that there are flowers only on your side of the path? I have always known about the crack. I planted those flower seeds and every day while we walk back, you water them. For two years I have been able to pick these beautiful flowers to decorate the table. Without you being just the way you are, there wouldn't be this beauty to grace the house."

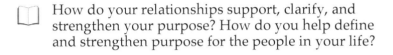 How do your relationships support, clarify, and strengthen your purpose? How do you help define and strengthen purpose for the people in your life?

In what ways do your relationships undermine or distract from your purpose? What would it take to bring them back into alignment?

🖐 Superstar

Think of your life like a Hollywood movie where you are the star and your relationships are the supporting cast. Who is in your movie? What parts of your purpose are supported by the relationships in your life? Who could you imagine coming into your life to help clarify and support your purpose? Spend some time imagining what it would look and feel like to be in collaboration around your purpose.

Step 11: Allowing

> *Whatever the present moment contains,*
> *accept it as if you had chosen it. Always work*
> *with it, not against it. This will miraculously*
> *transform your whole life.*
> Eckhart Tolle

"Allowing" is appreciating people and experiences *as they are* in the present moment. When we allow, we practice acceptance, and acceptance keeps us aligned with our reality. Allowing uses a new type of patience, releases control, and honors our own process of becoming our truest selves.

Allowing places us firmly in the present moment. It keeps us from spinning our wheels in resistance. In relationships, allowing means letting go of judgment and accepting what is, including our own feelings about it.

If we are truly practicing allowing in our relationships, we can accept what's true in our circumstances without judgment. We can acknowledge our own feelings about it without expecting that circumstances will change. And finally, we can choose for ourselves without needing to make the other person wrong. Allowing lets us love and accept others while maintaining the freedom to make our own choices.

> ***Replacing the need to control with the freedom***
> ***of allowing keeps relationships in alignment.***

Jason was recently faced with a challenging but inevitable life event. His father was told by his doctors that he needed to increase his dialysis treatments to three times a week in order to maintain his health. After much thought and discussion, his father decided it was time to discontinue dialysis and allow his body to begin shutting down.

When Jason first heard the news, he wanted his father to change his mind. Any sacrifice seemed reasonable to him if he could still have his father around.

However, instead of acting on his first instinct, he practiced allowing. Although Jason was sad, he wanted to respect his father's choice. By releasing the need to control the situation, he found peace in allowing his father to make the choice that was best for him. And by doing so, Jason was able to spend the precious time he had left with his father appreciating him and loving him as he is.

Where do you find allowing the hardest in your relationships?

Where is allowing easy? What makes it easy?

Hit the ESC Key

Think of one relationship where you are willing to practice allowing this week. What specific situation are you trying hard (and probably unsuccessfully) to control? This week, try letting go and simply allowing. Notice what's happening and allow your feelings without acting on them. What effect does it have on your relationship to simply allow what is?

Step 12: Listening

> *There was a definite process by*
> *which one made people into friends; it*
> *involved talking to them and listening*
> *to them for hours at a time.*
> Rebecca West

Listening is an act of intent that requires attention, focus, and concentration. Listening attentively requires allowing others to speak without interrupting or interjecting your own thoughts. Listening is important because being heard fulfills a human need. When we are heard, we feel acknowledged and validated.

Listening creates deeper connections with others. We can tune in to people on multiple energetic levels if we are truly listening to them. Not only can we hear someone's words and tone, but we can observe their facial expressions and bodily gestures. We can connect to a person's emotions by opening our hearts and getting in touch with our intuition.

In relationships, listening shows respect. Listening allows people to think out loud and clarify their thoughts and concerns. Listening requires patience, and the gift of our time is an act of kindness. Becoming an effective listener helps you and another person to align with each other's thoughts and allows for a deeper and more meaningful connection.

Becoming an active listener keeps you better aligned with others in your relationships.

My friend Chad and I both enjoy many of the same things—good food, good music, and good stories. One of our favorite activities is a good debate. We are both very passionate, and our debates are lively, energetic, and spirited. Since we're both also a bit stubborn, we constantly find ourselves challenging one another—even if we agree.

The key to our productive debates is our ability to listen to each other completely. Chad and I have learned how to be patient and allow the other person to complete his pontification in detail—no matter how long it takes. Many times, hubris leads us to believe we know the point being made, but we are often mistaken. We usually end up surprised by the conclusion—we actually learn something new! Thanks to listening, Chad and I can continue to have our lively debates. In fact, we look forward to them.

When is it important for you to listen deeply in your relationships? What do you gain when you do?

When have you been fully heard in your relationships? How does that experience affect the relationship?

Listen Up

The next time you're in a conversation, stop and give your full attention to the person speaking to you. Just be quiet and listen. Avoid the need to interrupt or speak when there is a pause in the conversation. Realize that they may be thinking a new idea or a summary, or they may even be having an epiphany. Don't speak over someone's moment of truth! Ask questions and become genuinely interested in what they have to say. You might be surprised by what you hear and maybe even more surprised by what you learn.

Step 13: Appreciation

*There is a calmness to a life lived
in Gratitude. . . a quiet joy.*
Ralph H. Blum

Appreciation is the act of expressing genuine gratitude and thanks. All human beings need to feel appreciated and valued. Appreciation can be expressed through acknowledgement, admiration, or approval. The gift of appreciation can be given freely and is seldom forgotten.

Appreciation is respect expressed. When we show our appreciation, we align ourselves with the love already inside us, and share it with others. We can appreciate all of the people in our lives—even the difficult ones. Even if we aren't sure what we gained, we can appreciate the lessons learned.

In relationships, it's beneficial to find a way to appreciate both similarities and differences. Contrasts in our relationships provide us with opportunities for growth. Being in a state of appreciation will always put you back into alignment with those whom you value in your present environment. Expressing authentic appreciation for others fosters collaboration and encourages continued partnership.

**Expressing genuine appreciation for others
helps us to stay aligned with one another.**

Julie was having difficulty at work. Her manager was always busy and didn't take the time to stop and really listen to her. Her coach asked her to list what she appreciated about her manager. At first, she was stumped. Then she remembered his presentation style. He could dazzle a room of people. With thought, she listed a few other attributes. Her coach suggested that Julie focus on the things she appreciated about her manager during her next meeting with him.

In only one month, Julie couldn't believe the change she experienced with her manager. The energy of their relationship had completely shifted. Now their meetings were productive and they were able to talk about things she'd been waiting months to discuss. Her feelings of appreciation for him brought their relationship back into alignment. Julie had learned firsthand how people respond to positive appreciation—even when it's not spoken aloud.

How does it feel when someone genuinely appreciates you? What effect does it have on your relationship?

What happens when you appreciate other people?

Treasure Hunt

Think about someone in your life who challenges you—a friend, family member, co-worker, boss—someone who is driving you crazy, or someone with whom you just don't get along. Now put that person in your mind's eye, and begin to think of something—anything—that you genuinely appreciate about them. There's buried treasure in there somewhere! Even if it takes a while, come up with a list of at least three things. Focus on those things that you appreciate about them the next time you speak with that person. Notice how this simple shift changes the relationship.

Step 14: Timing

> *To everything there is a season and a time*
> *to every purpose under the heaven.*
> The Bible, Ecclesiastes 3:1

Timing is a part of the cycles of life. The phrase "Timing is everything" highlights the importance of timing. If we trust that life has a divine and perfect timing, we can recognize that people and experiences are always brought to us when the time is right.

Our lives change and so do we. Time is fluid. Recognizing the divine syncopation of our world teaches us to practice patience while our intentions manifest. We can develop an appreciation for timing by recognizing when aspects of our lives are not in alignment and it "isn't the right time." These things can be added to a *waiting patiently* list.

Timing affects the life cycles of our relationships. Each relationship is unique. Some relationships last a short time, others last longer—some last our entire lifetime. As we change, so do our wants and needs, and our relationships reflect those changes. Loving someone means knowing when the timing is right to take a step further into intimacy or release the relationship in gratitude for what it has given us.

Alignment with purpose allows you
to respect the timing of relationships.

Susan and Tammy had been friends since college and remained friends after they had both married. They talked on the phone monthly and got together several times a year. Then their phone calls began to drop off. They saw each other less and less. Susan tried to connect with Tammy through email, voicemail, and even snail mail, without success. Susan eventually heard from another source that Tammy was having difficulties in her marriage. Susan felt hurt and wondered why Tammy didn't come to her for support.

A few more months went by without Susan hearing from Tammy. Susan knew it was time to let her frustration go. She recognized that people change and made the decision to release the need to know why Tammy had ended their friendship. Even though she didn't understand why, eventually Susan respected Tammy's decision and was able to look back on their relationship with appreciation.

How have your relationships been affected by timing?

When have you fought against the timing of a relationship? When have you been in the flow? How are these experiences different?

That Was Then, This is Now

Where are you struggling with timing in a relationship right now? What are you waiting for that isn't yet happening, or what are you resisting that is already in process? What would happen if you stopped waiting? What would happen if you let go of resistance? Accepting the timing in your relationships is just another way of accepting what is, now. This week, try to accept something you've been resisting and see what happens.

Exercise for Alignment: Tell Me More About That

This exercise is meant to be done with another person. It is an active listening exercise designed to assist you with developing better listening and communication skills.

Begin by choosing either a topic or story that both of you agree to discuss. If you're stuck, just ask the other person to tell you about their last vacation in detail. Set a timer for 15 minutes and allow the other person to start speaking. If they come up short on content, the only thing you are allowed to say is, "Tell me more about that."

While they are speaking, do not speak. Practice calming your thoughts and giving the speaker your full and undivided attention. Be sure to use direct eye contact and listen attentively to what they are *really* saying the entire time. Your thoughts should be only on them, their story, their words, emotions, and energy. If, at any point, you feel the need to comment, gently release the need to respond. Your job is only to listen. When the timer goes off, switch roles and repeat.

Speaker: How did it feel to be listened to uninterrupted? Did your mind wander or stay focused? Did you feel uncomfortable without any interaction from your listener?

Listener: How did it feel to listen and not comment or ask questions? Did you find your mind wandering or staying focused? If you lost focus, what could have helped you regain focus? Did you feel uncomfortable without any interaction with your speaker?

Listening is a skill that can be developed over time. Take the opportunity to become a good listener and notice how it improves balance in your relationships!

Chapter 6: The Key is Activation

*Taking a new step, uttering a new
word, is what people fear most.*
Dostoevsky

Awareness brings attention to the critical factors influencing our relationships; alignment helps us focus our energy by aligning with our deepest purpose; activation puts theory into practice and ideas into motion. Without activation, good ideas are only ideas. Activation is the key to implementation and the third stage to finding better balance in our relationships.

The next seven steps are opportunities for activation. Focusing on activation helps us make changes in our lives and reminds us that manifesting our truest purpose and our dreams both depend on our ability to take action.

Step 15: Begin Within

*We don't receive wisdom; we must
discover it for ourselves after a journey
that no one can take for us or spare us.*
Marcel Proust

We were all given the power to use our thoughts, feelings, and intuition to direct and manage our lives. Our intuition—the language of the spirit—is our connection to higher consciousness. Many of us experience intuition through a nudge or hunch, or a "gut" feeling—different and deeper than a typical emotional response.

To *begin within* is to return to ourselves and the spiritual voice within each of us. When we follow our inner nudges, we put ourselves in alignment with our deepest truths and begin the creative process from the inside out.

Begin within by paying attention to your intuition and begin taking action in connection with higher consciousness.

Many years ago, I was visiting my home town and wanted to find a massage therapist. As I flipped through the local phone directory, I saw an advertisement and suddenly felt a tingle in my stomach. The words, pictures, and layout of the advertisement told me this was the place. I called for an appointment and spoke with Kathleen. When I met Kathleen the next day, I felt like we had known each other our whole lives. My intuition told me this new friendship would change my life.

Over several years, Kathleen taught me the value of listening deeply to my intuitive nudges and giving them a voice through my feelings and words. Kathleen helped me get in touch with my truth, intentions, and power.

Her connection to the spiritual energetic world is so crystal clear that her alignment with her own truth set the example to help me come into alignment with mine.

My relationship with Kathleen has helped me to understand the importance of following my soul's calling and beginning within.

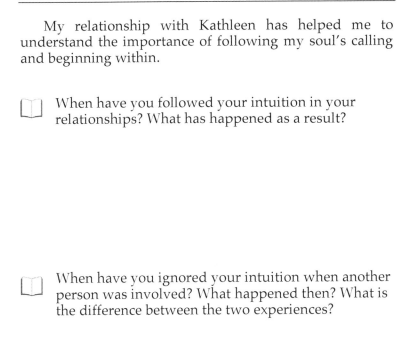 When have you followed your intuition in your relationships? What has happened as a result?

When have you ignored your intuition when another person was involved? What happened then? What is the difference between the two experiences?

Follow the Nudge

Where are you feeling a strong intuition in one of your relationships? What gut feelings are you ignoring or avoiding? How would you behave differently if you trusted your intuition? This week, focus on getting in touch with your intuition and applying it in your relationships. Listen to yourself and pay attention to the creative process that is constantly happening within you. Follow your nudges and notice the results.

Step 16: Walk in Their Shoes

Activation

> *Could a greater miracle take place that for us*
> *to look through each others' eyes for an instant?*
> Henry David Thoreau

If you've ever heard the phrase "Take a walk in my shoes," you knew the person saying it was asking you to see things from their perspective. Perspective is what we know and believe based on what we've previously experienced. If we take someone's perspective, we make an effort to understand what they know and believe based on their experience—without evaluation. This is how wisdom is passed forward.

Appreciating perspective keeps us open to making connections with people who have differing viewpoints, beliefs, and experiences. By integrating the perspectives of others, we practice compassion and deepen our relationships. When we seek to understand perspective, we create lasting and valuable connections. This builds a foundation of trust in new relationships and strengthens trust in existing ones.

Problem solving and collaboration are dependent on the ability to understand perspective. Taking the time to understand another's perspective and integrate it with our own mindset is a form of validation.

> *Activating perspective keeps you open to*
> *new understanding within relationships.*

"Why are you so happy all the time?" Jeff asked his Grandpa Walt. "Well, when you've been around the circuit as long as I have," replied Walt, "you see a lot of things come and go. . . and you learn pretty fast what's really important." It was another summer weekend at his Grandparents' cabin—an annual outing—and Jeff was bored already. I don't know why we have to come here every year, he thought. I'd rather be home hanging out with my friends.

Even though Jeff was 17, he thought he knew his Grandpa Walt pretty well. But Walt had recently been diagnosed with terminal lung cancer and was given six more months to live. "You've got to enjoy the people in your life, Jeff," Walt told him, "because you never know when they're going to be gone." Walt proceeded to tell Jeff about his cancer diagnosis and about how his own mother had died of cancer when he was only 17 years old—the same age as Jeff. Walt had always wished he would've appreciated his mother while she was alive. He never realized she would be gone so soon. After their conversation, Jeff asked if he could come and visit again next month. Grandpa Walt smiled. "Of course," he replied.

How are you actively valuing differing perspectives in your relationships?

In what ways can taking the time to learn a different perspective help bring better balance to your relationships?

These Shoes Were Made for Walking

The next time you are listening to someone, imagine their perspective. If they are providing their opinion, listen to their reasons for supporting their thoughts. If they are telling you a story, get in touch with how they are feeling as they tell it. Genuinely seek to understand them, their thoughts, and their feelings. Take a walk in their shoes; learn to truly appreciate their perspective; and notice how it strengthens your relationship.

Step 17: Choose For Yourself

Activation

> *If you choose not to decide,*
> *you still have made a choice.*
> Neal Pert, Rush, "Free Will"

Choice is our greatest gift. In choosing, we create our own unique experience. Each choice we make brings a different result, and our choices—like our experiences—are constantly changing. Our attitude, perspective, and behavior are choices, and when we change our minds, we create new choices.

Understanding and respecting the power to choose means learning that we ultimately can only choose for ourselves. Attempting to choose for others is a form of control that denies them the freedom to make their own choices. Sharing our opinions and perspectives when invited and without expectation allows others to still choose for themselves.

In relationships, we choose our level of commitment by considering the purpose and desired outcome of each relationship. This helps us to choose how much time and energy to invest. Our relationships are dynamic and constantly changing. One of the biggest roles choice plays in our relationships is recognizing and honoring that relationships have life cycles and choosing when to maintain, alter, or end them.

> *Activating your power of choice gives*
> *you the freedom to create your experience.*

A man and woman who had broken up a few years back ran into each other at the supermarket. They hadn't spoken in a long time, but for some reason they both felt the nudge to say hello. After a bit of chitchat, they both revealed that the relationships they pursued after their separation had failed. They admitted thinking about what would've happened if they'd stayed together. By the end of the conversation, they decided it would be nice to meet for coffee sometime and chat more.

When they met for coffee, they shared details about the changes they'd both experienced, observations on life, and what they had learned about themselves. They ended up talking and laughing for nearly four hours. By the end of the conversation they had reconciled their differences. Before they parted ways, the woman reached into her bag, took out a large envelope, and handed it to the man. Inside the envelope were thoughts and poems she had written to him after they had separated. Choices that had initially pushed them apart had also created the opportunity for them to reconnect.

When have you made a clear choice in your relationships? When have you chosen by *not* choosing? How have these experiences been different?

Where do you want to make a clearer choice before the circumstances change on their own?

Choose That, Not This

The next time you're faced with a decision—whether it's how to approach an important conversation, or even what to eat for lunch—think first what you would normally say or do, and then think again. Exercise your power of choice and choose something different. Even consider choosing something out of your comfort zone. Live a little! Notice how it feels to try something new. If you experience an undesirable outcome, now you know what *not* to choose. Either way, you learn.

Step 18: Befriend Your Family, Befamily Your Friends

A family is a circle of friends who love you.
Unknown

As adults, we make choices regarding whom we include in our lives. Many of us have grown up with parents, siblings, and other biological family members, but some of us haven't. Essentially, the term "family" can apply to anyone in your life who is important to you.

As we enter our adult lives, most of us leave home, create our own unique life space, and begin to fill it with new people. We form new groups consisting of our closest friends, a significant other, or sometimes even co-workers. These are the people we love, respect, and cherish most. These people become our new family.

For some adults, continuing their relationships with parents, brothers, and sisters is natural and an important part of their lives; for others, it is more difficult. Time and distance can make fathers into foreigners and siblings into strangers. If you choose, these relationships can be transformed with time and attention. Having your family as friends requires patience, perspective, and acceptance; but we can learn to communicate effectively, respect our differences, and agree to disagree.

Integrating friendships and family into
your life enriches your experiences.

It had only been two years since Ryan had graduated from college and moved cross-country to California, but he still was having difficulty "finding his feet." He had gotten a great job in sales, found a fantastic apartment by the ocean, and made a few new friends.

But Ryan still felt lonely. He had been very close to his parents and siblings back home in Wisconsin, but he could only afford to fly back and see them during the Christmas holidays. He really missed his family.

One day, Ryan's co-worker Mark asked him if he'd like to join a co-ed softball team. Ryan loved the idea, easily made the team, and quickly connected with the group. Within two months, Ryan and Mark had became close friends, and Ryan had started dating Mary—another softball player. Instead of spending Thanksgiving alone and wishing he was with his family, Ryan went with Mary and Mark to a gathering of friends—and felt surrounded by love, just like at home.

In what ways do you consider your friends as family and family as friends? In what ways are family and friends completely separate categories?

How has developing or ending relationships with your family brought you healthy and loving relationships with others?

All in the Family

Take time this week to think about the different people who have been a part of your life throughout the years. Think about your family of origin, your close friends, roommates, classmates, relatives, co-workers—anyone who has been a part of your life. Which of them felt like family? Which of them still do? Pause and appreciate that your family is as big as your experience. Appreciate each person for who they are and what they've contributed to your life.

Step 19: Soften Your Stance

Any intelligent fool can make things bigger, more complex,
and more violent. It takes a touch of genius—and a
lot of courage—to move in the opposite direction.
Albert Einstein

We are all gifted with powerful thoughts, feelings, and intuition. Taking time to listen to our intuition and choose responses to our thoughts and feelings wisely will increase our chances of experiencing harmonious interactions. To *soften your stance* is to step back from your natural impulse to speak or act with power and force and either choose a gentler response or none at all. Sometimes nothing is the best thing to say and often the best thing to do.

When we soften our stance, we become aware of the impact we have on those around us and learn to respond in appropriate and effective ways. Even when we are very passionate about something—which can create more intensity and enthusiasm—we can consciously choose to pause, breathe, and think before speaking or acting. By calming ourselves and resting in our perspective, we can choose how to respond to our thoughts and feelings with calm confidence.

Our interactions with others provide the best opportunities for us to learn about ourselves. Through observation and feedback, we can learn how to soften our stance and pay attention to our approach. We can learn to discern between impulse and intuition, see the bigger picture, and consider our options before our actions.

Soften your stance to give yourself
and others more room to connect fully.

Heidi is a well-respected and powerful senior manager of a Fortune 500 corporation. She has risen to the top of every team she's managed and is known to speak her mind when action is needed. Since she is a natural problem solver, people come to Heidi for solutions.

Over the years, however, Heidi began to feel overwhelmed, and her relationships with co-workers and supervisors became difficult and stressed.

When Heidi learned she could soften her stance, she had a personal epiphany. Her natural inclination was to be vocal and outspoken, but she realized that she didn't always need to share her thinking. Heidi realized she could pick and choose where and when to focus her energy. When she committed to *not* doing and saying her first impulse, others around her were able to step up. Within a month, Heidi's blood pressure went down, her happiness went up, and her relationships improved. Heidi discovered a new type of personal power.

In which areas of your relationships could you benefit from learning to soften your stance?

In what ways might softening your stance change your connections with others?

Get More Flies With Honey

Tired of pushing your pitch? Remember that we learn the most by sharing ideas through collaboration rather than collision. This week, pay attention to the next time you're asked to take action or you're trying to get your point across. Pause, think, and try softening your stance. Notice how it shifts your energy and the energy between you and others.

Step 20: Go With the Flow

The only way to make sense out of change is to
plunge into it, move with it, and join the dance.
Alan W. Watts

Change is constant in life. Sometimes change feels like it's happening *to* us, but change is happening *for* us—giving us the opportunity to recreate our perspective. If we have courage to move with change, we can go with the flow and become a part of it.

Many people struggle to find the balance between reacting to change and anticipating it. Becoming a leader of change requires us to re-evaluate our limitations and become flexible with the process. Change is a constant—we can either resist or accept it. If we choose resistance, change can be difficult, but with acceptance, change is expected.

Since relationships also follow the dynamic ebb and flow of life, *going with the flow* allows us to assist others to do the same with confidence and conviction. Being proactive begins with you.

Choosing to change allows you to accept the world outside of you.

Doug was laid off from a company where he'd been working for over ten years. Although the news was a shock to him, his first thought was how he was going to tell his fiancé. Doug and Amy had been saving their money for the past two years so they could get married. But now he wasn't sure of anything. He felt like the whole world had stopped. He couldn't imagine what he was going to do next.

That evening, Doug and Amy sat down to discuss the situation. While Amy listened, Doug expressed his anger and disappointment about losing his job, and his fear about what was going to happen next.

Amy shared a different perspective with him. "Do you realize this is an opportunity for something new?" she said. Over the next few days Doug realized he did, indeed, have many options. He decided to take things step by step and look at this change as a positive opportunity for new direction and growth. In time, Doug was able to find a new job that he loved which paid more than his last job. He learned that change can, indeed, be something to appreciate and not to fear.

How has resisting or embracing change affected your relationships?

In what ways could *going with the flow* bring better balance to your relationships?

Change It Up

Where are you resisting change? How would it be different if you accepted it, or even encouraged or facilitated it? This week, try changing something about your routine that you have been resisting. Notice how the new relationship with yourself affects your relationships with others.

Step 21: Enact Love

Activation

> *To give pleasure to a single heart by*
> *a single act is better than a thousand*
> *heads bowing in prayer.*
> Mahatma Gandhi

Love in action is the highest form of love. If you've heard the phrase "Actions speak louder than words," then you know the important role that action takes. Thinking loving thoughts is a great start; feeling love in your heart is even better; speaking and acting out of love is as good as it gets.

Love in action takes many forms. The gift of your time and attention is love in action. Showing your interest is love in action. Listening with an understanding heart is love in action. Telling someone how much they mean to you is love in action. Standing by a friend when times are tough is love in action. When you demonstrate love in action, you seek the best in all situations; you encourage and support others unconditionally.

Love in action provides mutual benefits—both the giver and receiver benefit by the joy that love produces. When we act from love, we reconnect with the love in ourselves, and this keeps our frequency in alignment with a state of peace and joy. When love comes first, actions will follow.

> **Activation of the love within you creates**
> **loving attitudes, actions, and words.**

One year at the Special Olympics, nine contestants assembled at the starting line for the 100-yard dash. At the gun they all started out, not exactly in a dash, but with the goal to run the race, finish, and win. All, that is, except one boy who stumbled a couple of times, fell, and began to cry.

The other eight runners heard the boy cry, slowed down, and paused. Then they all turned around and went back—every one of them.

One girl with Down Syndrome bent down, kissed the boy on the head, and said, "This will make it better." Then two of them helped him up, all nine linked arms, and walked together to the finish line. Everyone in the stadium stood and cheered for ten minutes.

How are you thinking, acting, and speaking in loving ways in your relationships?

What might be some ways you can increase loving thoughts, actions, and words to bring more balance and harmony in your relationships?

Act Up

Take time this week to send someone you love a card, email, or text message, or pick up the phone and tell them how important they are to you. If you're comfortable telling them you love them, then go ahead. Otherwise, think loving thoughts and speak loving words—choose words that uplift and encourage. Feel how much love is a part of your relationships and the important role it plays in keeping those connections strong.

Book Three

21 Keys to Work/Life Balance

Unlock Your Full Potential

Introduction

Do what you love and love what you do, for what you do most says most about you.

A recent study from Cox Media Group found that 89 percent of Americans view their work and life balance as a significant problem. Whether it's due to the expansion of technology or the plethora of choices that we face each day, our ability to filter information and stay focused is a constant challenge. The speed of our world is accelerating at an exponential rate and it doesn't appear that it will slow down any time soon. It's no wonder that it becomes more and more difficult to balance priorities between family, friends, and personal obligations while supporting our careers.

You have the potential to make healthy choices and balance your priorities no matter where you are on your life journey. However, change doesn't come easily—it takes courage, dedication, and commitment. Lasting change comes in small steps. Each step evolves into a new habit, and over time, healthy habits become major life changes. By seeking to understand yourself better, learning to focus your energy, and practicing new healthy habits, you can find a better balance of your work and life.

Remember: The power to make changes in your life is *always* in your hands. Make a commitment to paying closer attention to your priorities at work and at home and create the momentum for better work/life balance in your life today. It's your choice.

Chapter 7: Welcome to Awareness

To become different from what we are,
we must have some awareness of what we are.
Eric Hoffer

We are always learning. Our powerful consciousness is absorbing and processing everything in our environment—including information, sights, sounds, and smells—whether we realize it or not. From our experiences we make choices using the power of our thoughts, feelings, and intuition. In order to find better work/life balance, we must first become aware of the factors that influence our lives on a daily basis.

The first seven keys focus on awareness. Raising our awareness reminds us that the power to influence our work/life balance always begins with noticing what's happening in the present moment.

Key 1: The Balance Myth

Awareness

> *There is no secret to balance.*
> *You just have to feel the waves.*
> Frank Herbert

Is there really such a thing as work/life balance? Many say it's a myth. Balance implies harmony or equilibrium among *opposing elements.* Imagine what this looks like on a scale—work and life are not only separated, but at opposite ends of the spectrum. In this way, the idea of "work/life balance" supports the idea that work and life are separated. This myth of separation is supported by our environments. Since most people leave their home to go to work each day, the differences between work and home environments shift our energy and force us to refocus.

Now consider a different picture. Visualize your life as a circle with work as one of many different circles contained within it. All of our thoughts, feelings, and actions are constantly flowing in and out of these circles—now work and life are not opposing elements but rather work is one element in a much larger "life." Work is a part of life. The two elements are integrated. The answer to finding better work/life balance is to find the right blend between all our life activities—regardless of where and when they occur.

A true balance between work and life
comes with knowing that your life
activities are integrated, not separated.

Janelle felt like she was always behind. Her office was so different than her quiet home. It was no wonder she often had to stay late to get all her work done. When she first started her job five years ago, her team was very small—only seven people. But Janelle's team had grown to 24 and she felt like she was slowly sinking.

When Janelle got a new boss, Barbara, things changed. Barbara suggested that Janelle consider working from home a day or two a week.

Whereas Janelle's former boss had never supported working remotely, Barbara trusted her employees and understood the value of flexibility.

Working remotely helped Janelle to minimize distractions and maximize her productivity. The blend of working partly in the office and partly at home helped Janelle learn a new type of discipline—one that increased her productivity by helping her stay more focused when she worked from home. After only a month on the new schedule, Janelle found that coming to the office was more enjoyable. Things changed for the better. She had finally found the right blend.

How does your current focus at work and home balance out? What's working well? What's not?

What are some things you are doing to create a better blend between your work and life?

One + One

This week, write down one thing you'd like to *stop* doing and one thing you'd like to *start* doing to help bring better balance between your work and home life. For example, *I will stop checking my email every ten minutes*, and, *I will start taking a 30-minute walk each day*. Put this list where you can see it—on your laptop, iPad, desktop, or sticky note in your car—and make a commitment to changing *only* those two things this week.

Key 2: Choice

Awareness

> *I believe that we are solely responsible for our choices,*
> *and we have to accept the consequences of every deed,*
> *word, and thought throughout our lifetime.*
> Elisabeth Kubler-Ross

Choice is one of our most powerful gifts. Each choice we make brings a different result, and our choices—like our experiences—are constantly changing. Our attitude, perspective, and behavior are choices. In the words of Dennis S. Brown, "The only difference between a good day and a bad day is your attitude." There is tremendous power in perspective. By reframing our perspective, problems can be turned into opportunities.

Our actions are choices. We are all naturally reactive, because the human brain is designed to protect the body from harm. Reacting is natural, but responding is thoughtful. We can't always choose what happens to us, but we can choose how we *respond* to it. Our ability to adapt and evolve with change is also a choice. Resistance to change can create the illusion of fewer choices while accepting change will create opportunities for more choices.

Our choices decide our direction and carve a path for our personal lives and our careers. Establishing a healthy work/life balance includes the awareness that we can filter, prioritize, and plan our activities. By being selective about where we place our focus, we take control of our choices. Whatever we pay attention to expands—whether it is creative ideas or problems. The good news is that no matter the result of our choices, we can always choose again.

Being aware of the choices you make gives
you the freedom to create your own experience.

Each new year, Tim would promise to start a new exercise routine but could not keep the motivation to follow through with it. But this year he decided he was going to stick with it.

To help him stay motivated, Tim took the advice of a co-worker and hired a personal trainer to help him get started. After the first two weeks, Tim had a workout routine personally tailored to his body type and fitness goals.

After the first month, Tim found his personalized fitness plan was key to his motivation. But Tim also began to notice something else—he started making other healthy choices. As his body began to adjust to the physical exercise, he started craving healthier foods. Because he was eating healthier foods, Tim's weight began to shift. His attitude improved and his stress level was decreasing. As a result of his better mood, work started to flow with a new ease and Tim's relationships started to improve, especially with his wife. Tim had never realized how many aspects of his life were connected to his physical health and well-being. Tim quickly realized that one healthy choice can lead to so many more.

How have your choices affected your overall health and well-being at home? At work?

In what ways can you use your power to start choosing something different?

Choose Consciously

Take a moment this week to prioritize two important things: tasks and people. Take a short inventory of your tasks and ask yourself: Which tasks do I need to spend more time on? Where should I reduce my time? Now take inventory of your relationships: Whom do I need to spend more time with? From whom do I need to detach or take a step back? Add these decisions to your calendar or to-do list for the coming week.

Key 3: Intention

> *Don't confuse having a career with having a life.*
> Hillary Rodham Clinton

Intention is the direct reflection of our deepest truth and belief systems. Our intentions form the foundation for our attitudes, actions, and words. Intentions move our values from thought into word, word into action, and action into being.

Finding the true heart of our intention starts by asking ourselves what we really want. Sometimes this is clearest when we are experiencing what we *don't* want! Contrasting our experiences helps us to create what we *do* want. In fact, some of our most powerful intentions are born in our moments of greatest contrast.

Whether it is setting goals for work or personal life, intentions are more than just wishful thinking. In order for intentions to manifest, you have to take action. The act of speaking our intentions out loud shifts them from dreaming to doing. When we express a thought or feeling or take action, something always happens. When we discuss our intentions, we plant the seeds for collaboration and co-creation.

> **Becoming aware of your intentions helps you
> focus your priorities and create desired results.**

Jill wanted to make a lot of money. "Why not?" she thought. Jill had never really had a lot of money, and she believed that with the right opportunity she could use her education and skills to land a really good job. Sure enough, Jill landed a consulting job that paid more than twice as much money as she'd ever made before. The job was a road warrior position—up to 100% travel—but if that was the price to pay for making a whopping salary, then so be it. Her husband and friends would understand. What an opportunity! And yes, an opportunity it was—a chance for Jill to learn a very valuable lesson.

The first two months were hectic, although feasible. But by the end of six months the job was horrendous. Jill was working 65 to 70 hours a week, was only able to travel home for one day every two weeks, and was missing her husband. She had gotten a cold she just couldn't shake. The enormous paychecks sat mostly idle in Jill's bank accounts while she scrambled to keep up. By the time her seventh month came around, Jill was ready to quit. What had she been thinking when she took this job? The money. Was it worth her stress? Her health? Her marriage and friends? Jill had to reconsider her intentions.

How do your intentions support you in your current job? In your personal life?

In what ways could clarifying your intentions help create desirable outcomes?

Mention Your Intention

Intentions take life when we speak them out loud or write them down. Take a moment this week to think of your intentions for your career and your personal life, write them down, and then share them with someone you trust. Throughout the week, notice how your attitudes, actions, and words are either helping to fulfill your intentions or moving you away from them. If needed, make necessary changes to put yourself back on track.

Key 4: Frequency

> *You do not attract what you want.*
> *You attract what you are.*
> Dr. Wayne Dyer

Our frequency is defined as our personal energetic level. Our personal frequency is powerful, adjustable, and highly influenced by our state of mind, mood, and environment.

Words, body language, and facial expressions tell us about others' frequencies. We might refer to these observations as good or bad vibes. Being around someone who raises our frequency, or lifts our mood, feels much different than someone who "brings us down." When we meet people whose frequency is similar to ours, we tend to connect with them easily—we say we're "on the same wavelength." Being around people whose frequency is different from ours may cause us to feel awkward or uncomfortable.

In our personal lives, we tend to surround ourselves with people whose energies are most compatible with ours. Integrating personal frequencies in the workplace can be challenging, since we are less able to choose the people we work with. We may need to adjust our personal frequency to blend harmoniously with our work environment and the frequencies of the people in it.

> **Awareness of your frequency and the**
> **frequencies of others moves you to**
> **monitor and adjust frequency as needed.**

Holly is naturally social, wittily clever, and charming. In her last job, she had been on a team of like-minded project managers, and they had all grown accustomed to joking around with each other throughout the work day.

Holly had recently moved to a new city and accepted a job as a project manager with a new company. During her first week, she realized that most members of her new project team—especially her team leader—were very serious and professional in their interactions.

At first, Holly was disappointed. With her new team presenting such a contrasting vibe, she felt like she couldn't be herself. Then Holly realized that by gently adjusting her frequency, could learn to mesh with this new team. She started watching her words more carefully and became more conscious of her professionalism in the office. It felt strange at first, but after she got over her disappointment, it wasn't so bad. After her second week, several of Holly's teammates invited her to a happy hour. It was there she could relax and be more fun and playful with them, finding the right balance for her natural energy.

What do you know about your personal frequency? When do you need counter-balancing from others?

What do you notice about the frequencies of the people in your workplace? How can adjusting your frequency help you to blend better with others?

Do You Hear That?

This week, pay attention to the frequencies around you. What does it feel like when someone's frequency is similar to yours? What happens when someone's frequency is not like yours? How do you adjust to people's different frequencies? Write an example in your journal this week about how the frequency of someone else played an important role in contributing your sense of balance or lack of balance.

Key 5: Strengths

Balance, peace, and joy are the fruit of a successful
life. It starts with recognizing your talents and
finding ways to serve others by using them.
Thomas Kinkade

Strengths refer to our talents, skills, and abilities. Strengths can be discovered by becoming aware of what we naturally do well, or they can be identified through assessment tools. With education and experience, strengths can also be learned and developed over time. Becoming aware of our strengths and how to use them in our work and life leads us toward better work/life balance.

As many aspects of our personal lives overlap into work, our strengths can play a key role in bridging the gap between our job and home life. In the workplace, combining our strengths with the strengths of others fosters cooperation. True creativity blooms with collaboration.

Putting our strengths into action can instill a sense of purpose and increase feelings of confidence, self-esteem, and a desire to do more. When our strengths are recognized by others, we feel valued and appreciated.

Becoming aware of your strengths helps
you identify, develop, and share them.

Daniel enjoyed his job as field technician. Every week he was out on the road helping clients solve their technical problems. Over the years, Daniel had built a foundation of solid relationships with his clients and was continually bringing in new business. When it came time for Daniel's boss to retire, Daniel was recommended to take his place. Daniel reluctantly accepted the position because he thought it might offer him a chance to learn new skills.

Within two weeks of starting in his new position, Daniel was feeling completely out of his element. The manager's job was entirely different from his position as a field technician.

He was in the office five days a week and his meetings were only with other executives and the people he managed. After completing a strengths assessment, Daniel discovered his biggest strength was not managing people, but interacting with customers. Daniel decided to meet with the CEO and ask for his old job back. Fortunately, another candidate was still available for the manager's position, and Daniel went back to his old job. Daniel realized how being aware of his strengths had allowed him to be in a position that nurtured his well-being.

How has being aware of your strengths helped you in your job? In your personal life?

What strengths do you have that you're not using? Why not? What do you think would happen if you focused on them?

Creative Challenge

This week, think of something that you enjoy doing and that you do well. How often do you have the chance to do it? How can you add more of it to your work and life? For example, if you like graphic design and it's not part of your job, perhaps you can add some graphics to your status reports, presentations, or meeting agendas? Or maybe there's a chance for you to use your talents in a special event or project? Be willing to see how creative you can be about integrating your strengths and talents into what you already do.

Key 6: Power Awareness

> *What it lies in our power to do,*
> *it lies in our power not to do.*
> Aristotle

Power is the possession of authority, control, or influence over others. Personal power means having control over yourself—having the ability to make significant choices for yourself. *Power-over* involves having authority over other people and making significant choices for them. For example, there are many choices that parents make for their children because adults are more knowledgeable and capable than children. *Power-with* involves using power with others through efforts such as collaboration or negotiation toward a common goal.

People have different kinds of power in different situations. Sometimes it is implicit in a system or relationship, as when a manager has responsibility for the work done by others. We demonstrate power through our attitudes, actions, and words. Power can be used, consciously or unconsciously, either to manipulate and abuse or to support and encourage.

Balanced power is demonstrated through behaviors that lead, engage, and support. An imbalance of power may be evidenced by the use of criticism, bullying, or anger. Power can be best used by choosing carefully where to place our focus and realizing what's most important: the process or the outcome.

> ***Awareness of your power allows you***
> ***to also honor the power of others.***

Sharon's boss was out of touch with her power. Lillian was well-educated, socially savvy, and professionally astute. She had learned very early that her personal power was a key to her career success. However, now that she was Vice President of her division, she didn't know how to transform her power into support and encouragement.

She micro-managed many of Sharon's activities, leaving Sharon feeling frustrated and powerless.

Sharon's awareness that Lillian was out of touch with her power gave her a place to start in transforming their relationship. Sharon made it her intention to stay in a spirit of collaboration, and even though she didn't agree with all of Lillian's ideas, she started to work *with* her out of compassion instead of *against* her out of anger. Sharon found that if she didn't push against Lillian, she could gradually introduce ideas that would complement rather than challenge her. Over time, they were both able to achieve the results they wanted and Sharon no longer felt overpowered.

How does power show up in your relationships at work? At home? How are they similar or different?

When do you experience the most personal power? How does that affect the rest of your life?

Power Play

Think of a time when you felt powerful. What happened? What were you doing? Who were you with? If the memory was a personal experience, imagine translating that same feeling of power to a work experience or vice-versa. Now what does it feel like? What are you doing? Who are you with? What would it take for you to feel more powerful in this area of your life? What would you do or say differently? How can you apply this experience to change the balance of power in your life this week?

Key 7: Know Thyself

Awareness

> *I am larger, better than I thought.*
> *I did not know I held so much goodness.*
> Walt Whitman

The words "Know Thyself" were inscribed on the entrance to the Temple of Apollo at Delphi thousands of years ago. The ancient Greeks knew that recognizing your potential and learning from your life experiences was valuable, and this continues to be essential today. Knowing yourself is knowing that you are comprised of a mind, body, and spirit—that you have powerful thoughts, feelings, and intuition—and that you are continually creating your experience.

To know yourself is to love and accept yourself *as you are*—even though there are things you strive to improve. Knowing yourself involves being willing to recognize patterns of behavior that aren't working and being willing to change those patterns. When you focus on improving yourself, others in your life will also benefit. Happiness and well-being are contagious. People like seeing others happy and healthy—it can inspire them to make changes themselves.

When you know yourself—your strengths, joys, limitations, and fears—you can live in truth and transparency in all areas of your life. You can be your authentic self at home and bring yourself to work each day. When you know that you have worth and value, others also believe in you.

> **Knowing yourself means becoming aware**
> **of your potential and trusting that**
> **you are always growing into it.**

Ted was offered an opportunity to study abroad in Spain for graduate school. He had never traveled outside of the continental United States and he wasn't fluent in Spanish by any means, so this opportunity appeared to be a fantastic way for him to learn more about the Spanish culture.

Besides, it would be paid for by his graduate scholarship.

Ted had always been confident of himself and comfortable with his surroundings—but in Spain, he felt like a fish out of water. Being naturally social, he wanted to go out and party with other students but realized that most nights they were either studying or busy with their families. Ted was finding it hard to fit in until he was asked to play the part of an American tourist in a theater production—something he'd never done before. During rehearsals and performances, he ended up meeting new friends in the cast who taught him about Spanish culture. After returning, Ted realized how much the whole experience had expanded him; he felt that he would benefit from those lessons his entire lifetime.

In what ways could you know yourself better? What parts of you seem undeveloped, hidden, or mysterious?

In what ways are you taking care of yourself? How are you neglecting yourself?

Me Time

This week, schedule some time on your calendar for yourself—"me time." During this time, focus your energy on *yourself*. Allow yourself to drift into whatever you want—just don't do what you'd consider "work." Instead, read a book, go for a walk, listen to music, watch a movie—do something for yourself. As my good friend and fellow coach Honoree Corder says, "If it's not on the calendar, it's not happening!" Notice how time for yourself affects your sense of balance and equilibrium.

Chapter 8: Moving Into Alignment

*Tug on anything at all and you'll find it
connected to everything else in the universe.*
John Muir

Moving into alignment is the second stage to finding better work/life balance. Alignment happens both inside and outside of us. As we move in and out of alignment with our deepest self, our surroundings directly reflect our present state of balance. If we stay connected to our thoughts, feelings, and intuition, we understand more clearly what our true alignment is and find that alignment more easily.

The next seven keys will help you take a closer look at alignment. Focusing on alignment reminds us that a major influence on our work/life balance is the ability to consciously bring ourselves into alignment with the people and places that connect us with our deepest sense of purpose.

Key 8: Communication

Alignment

> *I've never regretted the things I said nearly*
> *as much as the words I left unspoken.*
> Lisa Kleypas

Through communication, we interact with others, sharing beliefs, values, and intentions. Words, though powerful, are only a small part of communication. We also communicate through our tone, expressions, and body language. Technology has improved our access to communication tools by offering speed and efficiency, often at the expense of clarity and mutual understanding. This is only one of many reasons why effective communication is important, especially in both work and personal environments.

In order to communicate in healthy and balanced ways, we must pay attention to how we are feeling and how our communication is received. By acknowledging our feelings and listening carefully before we speak, we can choose our words wisely and respond to others clearly and calmly.

When our communication is clear and honest, we are in alignment with our deepest intentions. When we ask questions and listen as much as we speak, we can find better balance in our connections with others both at work and in our personal lives.

Effective communication facilitates better alignment
between what you say and what you mean.

After an extensive remodel of their offices, a team of corporate professionals moved back into their building. During their first week, Tom, one of the team managers, was in the copy room trying to figure out how to operate their new all-in-one printer. A very important report had been given to him by a senior executive, and he needed to make copies for a meeting that afternoon.

By the time Debbie, the administrative coordinator, saw him, he had stepped away from the printer and set his report on the machine next to him—the new shredder. "Need some help?" Debbie asked. "Yes," replied Tom. "Do you know how this thing works?" "Sure. It's easy," Debbie said. She picked up the report and fed it into the shredder.

When we fail to communicate effectively, we miss the message. Communication is, indeed, a two-way street.

How is your communication different at work than in your personal life? How is it similar?

How can your personal communication style be clearer and more effective?

Talk To Me

Strengthen your communication this week by becoming a good speaker or a good listener. Find a friend, co-worker, or family member and tell them that you are practicing communication skills. If you are naturally a talker, then you will only listen. If you are already a good listener, then you will only speak. Set a timer for 15 minutes and have either you or the other person speak uninterrupted for the entire 15 minutes. The subject can be anything at all. If you are the listener, do not speak—listen attentively. If you are the speaker, let your ideas and thoughts flow. What did you notice? How did this exercise affect the rest of your communication this week?

Key 9: Boundaries

Respect yourself and others will respect you.
Confucius

Boundaries are the seen and unseen rules of engagement necessary for protection, safety, and respect. Boundaries are often identified when they've been crossed or violated.

Creating and maintaining healthy boundaries demonstrates respect for ourselves and others and builds trust in both our work and personal relationships. Boundaries are different for every person and are developed by personal experiences. Underdeveloped or "blurred" boundaries may manifest in indecisiveness, aggression, or a need to control others.

Professional boundaries are dictated by the environment in which we are working—the culture and ethics of the business, the people, and the mission of the organization. Explicit boundaries can come in the form of rules and regulations (i.e., standards, policies, procedures), or agreements (i.e., contracts). Honoring professional boundaries demonstrates respect for the business and the people in it.

Developing personal and professional boundaries demonstrates respect for yourself and others.

Kathy had a conundrum. Her company was defending against a very large lawsuit brought by a former client, and several of the top executives were scrambling to make sure all of their bases were covered. Kathy was the executive assistant to the Vice President of Audit, and although she got along well with Ron, she wasn't always in agreement with his business ethics. The Audit department was always in the "hot seat" when it came to investigations of the company, and Kathy had waded her way through plenty of difficult situations in the past.

But this one was different. Kathy was being asked to do something she'd never done—to shred classified documents.

When she was first asked to shred the documents, Kathy questioned the actions but assumed it was part of proper procedure—just not one she'd done before. But something about it didn't feel right. Upon additional research, Kathy realized she was being asked to do something illegal. Her personal ethics were at stake. She discussed her feelings with Ron, but he wasn't sympathetic. He was in hot water. Kathy felt that compromising her integrity was out of the question—this would only become a slippery slope. Very sad about the whole situation, Kathy finally decided to resign from her position. Her boundaries had been challenged and crossed. Kathy had learned a valuable lesson in ethics by living it.

How have you established your personal boundaries at work? In your personal life?

Where do your boundaries need strengthening? Where could your boundaries be more flexible?

That's My Limit

Take a moment to think about a recent situation at home or work where you felt your boundaries were crossed. What happened? How did you react and what was the result? Now think of a time when you pushed someone to their limit and they let you know. How did you know that you crossed their boundary? What happened after that, and how did it change your relationship? Add these insights to your journal.

Key 10: Environment

*Our environment, the world in
which we live and work, is a mirror of
our attitudes and expectations.*
Earl Nightingale

Environment is one of the biggest influences on our work/life balance. Environment includes our physical surroundings as well as the people in them. Environment has a direct influence on our personal frequency. Work and home environments influence us in different ways, affecting the words we use, the clothes we wear, and the activities we engage in.

Environments trigger what's going on inside of us. If our current environment does not harmonize with our frequency, we can change it, adapt to it, or create our own environment. For example, if the noise in your neighborhood or office is driving you nuts, consider wearing earphones. In the workplace, many employees have found it possible to change their environments by encouraging their companies to provide things like flexible schedules, remote working opportunities, and more personal time off.

*To change your work/life balance,
consider changing your environment.*

Paul was excited about his new job. After working for a large multinational corporation for eight years, he had decided to leave the posh corporate life and return to small business. The corporate environment—powerful and fast-paced—had been very good to Paul, but it no longer appealed to him. He missed the ability to exercise his entrepreneurial passions, something that a large business didn't have room for but a small business would encourage.

The first few months in his new job were quite an adjustment.

Paul had forgotten about many of the things he'd taken for granted—solid structure; defined processes; teams and full departments that were led by a single person in the new company.

But after time for adjustment, Paul was feeling a different type of personal power. His job was to create an entirely new department, and the opportunity to "call his own shots" was worth the pay cut he took in order to accept the position. For Paul, growing and maturing meant returning to something simpler and smaller in scale.

Which things in your present work environment are supporting you? Which aren't? What about in your home environment?

How could you shift your environments, even just a little, so that they better support your intentions?

Here Today, Gone to Maui

Take a moment to remember your last trip away from home. It could've been a long vacation to a far away destination, or just a weekend away. Where did you go? What did you do? Why did you take this trip? Now reflect on how the contrast of that environment shifted your perspective. Did you feel relief? Or perhaps you felt uncomfortable being away from home? And when you returned from your trip, how did you feel? Relaxed? Refreshed? When you change your environment, your environment changes you. This week, think about how a shift in your environment—whether small or large—will affect you.

Key 11: Purpose
Alignment

> *People take different roads seeking fulfillment*
> *and happiness. Just because they're not on your*
> *road doesn't mean they've gotten lost.*
> Dalai Lama

A sense of purpose—knowing why we are here—helps give our lives meaning and contributes to an overall sense of worthiness. When our intentions are in alignment with our purpose, this is reflected in our choices and behaviors.

The different roles we play in work and personal life can become our different faces—each with a distinct purpose to fulfill. Our interactions and relationships with others outside work can feed our purpose. When our work is in alignment with our gifts and talents, it can also bring a deep sense of purpose. Our career can feel like a direct extension of a higher sense of purpose when we believe that what we do is part of a larger plan that is supporting us to step into our full potential.

> *Feeling alignment with a higher sense of purpose*
> *gives direction to your work and personal life.*

Sheila had always wondered why she was drawn to jobs in customer service. She knew that she enjoyed people and solving problems, and her cheerful attitude and friendly disposition were always appreciated by her customers, but Sheila longed for something more—a deeper meaning and feeling of purpose to her work. Due to downsizing, Sheila was unexpectedly laid off from her customer service job. While attending a job fair, she stopped by the booth representing the Department of Motor Vehicles (DMV). Like many others, Sheila dreaded visits to the DMV with its long lines, excessive waiting, and busy counter staff. The woman at the booth appeared very friendly and polite. Sheila thought this was unusual.

Then Sheila realized something important. Maybe her cheerful personality and friendly disposition was something they needed at the DMV. Wouldn't she want her own experience to be a positive one?

So Sheila applied, and sure enough, she was hired. Within the first two weeks of employment at a local DMV office, Sheila had received two customer compliments to her manager claiming that she was the kindest clerk they'd ever experienced. Sheila realized that her higher purpose was to be her cheerful self, and that the places that needed her most were the best places for her to be.

How often do you feel a sense of purpose? How does your current job support, clarify, and strengthen your purpose?

What can you do to strengthen your sense of purpose in your career? In your personal life?

Purpose Points

Stop and think about the last time you felt a strong sense of purpose. Perhaps it was when you were assigned a very important task, or maybe it was to be of support to someone when they needed it. This week, recognize and make note of those experiences where you feel a sense of purpose and be grateful for those moments. Write them down in a gratitude journal or make a thankful list.

Key 12: Relationships

Our greatest joy and our greatest pain
come in our relationships with others.
Stephen R. Covey

Relationships are the foundation for growth and expansion. Our relationships are an integral part of our personal and professional lives and help us to define and demonstrate who we really are. People are naturally wired to connect and collaborate with others. In relationship, we assist one another in creating our own life experience.

Relationships are the heart-centered connection between individuals. All healthy relationships are based on the core principles of trust, respect, and freedom. Unhealthy relationships result in criticism, control, abuse, or neglect. Healthy relationships are always entered into by choice and are based in freedom, not obligation.

Relationships are an essential ingredient to a healthy work/life balance. Relationships are about building networks. Developing groups of caring and supportive people from both your personal and professional lives provide you with resources to turn to for help, advice, and support when you need it. When you come into alignment with yourself, others will come into alignment with you.

Developing and nurturing healthy
relationships brings you into alignment
with others at work and in your personal life.

After many years of hoping and dreaming to find a job in Hawaii, Kim finally secured a job as a schoolteacher on the island of Kauai, the oldest of the Hawaiian Islands. Kim had only visited Hawaii once before she moved, but that was enough—she fell in love with the weather, the quiet lifestyle, and especially the people.

Kim had received a warm welcome when she had visited the islands two years before, and she knew that living there was going to be a wonderful experience.

After Kim had started her first week on the job, her principal invited her to a *pau hana*—an after-work happy hour—with the other teachers from her school. The faculty wanted to welcome her into their Hawaiian "ohana"—the word for family—an important step in the welcoming process for new employees. It became clear to her that relationships were central in Hawaiian culture. Soon she felt at home in her new job and new environment. At her new job, Kim made some of her closest friendships, for which she was always grateful.

How are your relationships at home and work serving you? How are they similar? How are they different?

What changes could you make in your relationships to bring them into closer alignment with your intentions and purpose?

Pass It On

Think of a relationship that's had a powerful impact on you and your life. This person may be a teacher, coach, friend, or parent—someone whose words or actions have made a lasting impression on you. Next, write down what you received from them. For example, in my life I was uplifted and encouraged by my high school music teacher, Mrs. Bradley. Mrs. Bradley believed in me and my talents, taught me to express my creative and musical self with confidence, and allowed me the opportunity to let my light shine for others to see. Repeat this exercise thinking of other people who've had significant impact on your life.

Key 13: Trust

Sometimes you cannot believe what you see;
you have to believe what you feel.
Mitch Albom

Trust, the foundation for all healthy and balanced relationships, involves believing in someone's reliability, integrity, competence, or strength. Trust is measurable and observable—it can be learned and taught.

Trust is developed and communicated through attitudes, actions, and words. Trust may be earned easily or developed over time. When you learn to trust and believe in yourself—your thoughts, feelings, and intuition—you give others the opportunity to trust you.

Trust creates transparency in both personal and workplace relationships. Trust is built through personal relationships where there is mutual recognition, validation, and respect. Trust in the workplace is created by upholding confidentiality and other ethical business practices. Personal trust is also developed and strengthened through networks of friends and colleagues.

Developing trust in personal and professional
relationships strengthens your connections.

When I lived in India during 2007-2008, I learned about the value of trust. In India, people are very heart-centered and put great emphasis on making a very personal and emotional connection with others, especially if you are a foreigner. When you first meet an Indian, they will ask you very personal questions: where do you live, are you married, do you have children? Indians are very interested in getting to know who you are and what you are about. This personal connection to you helps build trust.

Likewise, in business, Indians prefer to learn more about you personally before they work with you professionally. The idea of "people before process" was something I learned quickly, and I was able to adapt to this style of connection.

Western culture does not have the same approach to business. Having a culture that encourages and supports connections between people creates an environment of trust and respect that can be the foundation for healthy personal and business relationships.

How does trust play a significant role in your current job? In your personal life? How do these levels of trust differ? How are they similar?

Where do you trust yourself, and where do you feel out of alignment with yourself?

In We I Trust

Take a moment this week to evaluate your relationships. Choose one area where you would like to a) develop more trust in someone; and b) behave in a more trustworthy way. Now list the ways in which the person in scenario a) IS trustworthy. What can you trust them for? Make a list of these things and add to it throughout the week. For scenario b), what can you be trusted for? Make a list and add to it throughout the week. Placing your attention on trust will help to develop it.

Key 14: Appreciation

*Among the things you can give and still keep
are your word, a smile, and a grateful heart.*
Zig Ziglar

Appreciation is the act of expressing genuine thanks. All human beings need to feel appreciated and valued. Appreciation can be expressed through acknowledgement, admiration, or approval. The gift of appreciation can be given freely and is seldom forgotten.

Like our attitude, expressing appreciation is a choice. When we show our appreciation, we align ourselves with the natural gratitude inside of each of us and share it with others. Everyone appreciates someone who is thankful. Expressing authentic appreciation for others fosters collaboration and encourages continued partnership. Appreciation at work begins as we acknowledge others for what they do and respect them for who they are.

Developing a spirit of appreciation creates an attitude of gratitude. We can learn to appreciate all of our experiences because even the difficult ones have a lesson for us to learn. If you want to feel more appreciation, appreciate what you already have and the people and circumstances around you.

**Appreciation puts you in alignment with
others and in alignment with yourself.**

Adam was frustrated at work. He felt that his manager never acknowledged him for the hard work he was doing. During a coaching session, Adam's coach asked him to take time and list what he appreciated about his manager. At first, he was stumped. Then he realized he had always respected his manager's ability to juggle multiple projects with difficult customers without losing his cool. With more thought, he listed a few other attributes.

His coach suggested that instead of focusing on what he didn't like, that Adam focus on the things he appreciated about his manager during his next meeting with him.

He didn't even need to tell him, just think of those attributes and see his manager in that light.

In only one month, Adam couldn't believe the change he experienced. The energy of their relationship had completely shifted. Their meetings became more productive and his manager started to recognize his work. Adam's feelings of appreciation for his manager brought their relationship back into alignment. He had learned firsthand how people respond to appreciation—even when it is not spoken aloud.

How does it feel when someone genuinely appreciates you at work? At home? What effect does it have on your confidence or self-esteem?

What happens when you show your appreciation for other people? How do you feel?

Treasure Hunt

Think about someone in your life who challenges you—a friend, family member, co-worker, boss—someone who is driving you crazy, or someone with whom you just don't get along. Now put that person in your mind's eye, and begin to think of something—anything—that you genuinely appreciate about them. Even if it takes a while, come up with a list of at least three things. There's buried treasure in there somewhere! Focus on those things the next time you speak with that person. With time and patience, notice how this simple act of unspoken appreciation changes your relationship.

Chapter 9: The Key is Activation

Nothing happens until something moves.
Albert Einstein

Awareness brings attention to the critical factors influencing our work/life balance; alignment helps us focus our energy; activation puts theory into practice and ideas into motion. Without activation, good ideas are only ideas. Activation is the key to implementation and the third stage to finding better work/life balance.

The next seven keys are opportunities for activation. Focusing on activation helps us make changes in our lives and reminds us that finding a healthy blend between our work and personal activities depends on our ability to take action.

Key 15: Begin Within

> *Do not go where the path may lead, go instead*
> *where there is no path and leave a trail.*
> Ralph Waldo Emerson

We were all given the power to use our thoughts, feelings, and intuition to direct and manage our lives. Intuition—the language of the spirit—is our connection to higher consciousness. Many of us experience intuition through a hunch, or a "gut" feeling—different and deeper than a typical emotional response. The voice of our intuition is quiet and often difficult to hear.

To *begin within* is to return to ourselves and the intuitive voice within each of us. When we follow our inner nudges, we put ourselves in alignment with our deepest purpose. Connecting with intuition teaches us to trust our deeper instincts. Following your intuition will always lead you to the best experience for your growth right now.

Many decisions in our work and personal lives require us to follow our intuition. Whether it is from our professional education and training or our upbringing, we all have experience to draw from. Adding our intuitive guidance to our thoughts and feelings gives us wisdom and courage to make decisions that are in alignment with our intentions. To begin within is to trust the process.

Begin within by listening to your intuition and trusting your instincts.

Karen couldn't decide what to do. Her good friend's husband had been recently diagnosed with cancer and hospitalized. Karen didn't know the husband very well, but her friend was important to her. Even though she couldn't be sure her friend would be at the hospital that morning, something was nudging Karen to stop by—even just for a quick visit. So Karen quickly signed a card and grabbed an inspirational magnet off her refrigerator and put it in with the card. She stopped by the hospital, and to her relief, her friend was there along with other family.

Two years later, Karen got a note that her friend's husband had suffered a recurrence, quickly deteriorated, and had died. Karen attended the funeral. After the service, Karen's friend approached her to thank her for coming to the service, and also to thank her for the card years ago. She said that the inspirational magnet had given her strength and hope over the two years between her husband's first illness and his death. Karen had completely forgotten about the magnet but realized that her intuitive nudge had helped her to give her friend courage during her husband's illness. Karen was thankful that she had followed her intuition.

When have you had an intuitive nudge about something or someone? How did you act on it? How did it turn out?

Where is your intuition leading you right now? What inner knowledge are you tempted to ignore?

Listen Up

This week, pay attention to your intuition. Whether you are engaged in a conversation at home or at work, focus on what your intuition is saying to you. If you are at work and sitting in a meeting, notice how there is an internal dialogue going on inside of you as well as the one outside of you. What are you thinking and feeling about the topic of discussion? What is your intuition telling you? Take a moment to jot down what comes to mind.

Key 16: Human Being, Human Doing

You find peace not by rearranging the circumstances of your life,
but by realizing who you are at the deepest level.
Eckhart Tolle

We are human beings. We contribute to our families, friends, co-workers and all other relationships by simply being ourselves. We are also human "doings." We have jobs and careers that produce a specific outcome; the income we receive is compensation for this effort. But we are not our jobs or careers—our work is only an extension of who we are. If we identify ourselves by our careers, then we lose the opportunity to step into our full potential.

The difficulty comes in separating "doing" from "being." Since our work is often defined by our role, what we are doing is more easily recognized than who we are being. When we say we are a doctor, a teacher, or a waitress, that is not who we *are*, that is what we *do*. Society places a large importance on what we do as a primary measure of our personal success. It is true that being productive is essential in the workplace, but work is only one of the small circles inside the big circle that is our life.

The truth is that we are connected beings and we have a need to be recognized and validated not only for what we do, but also for who we are. When there is a connection made between our personality and productivity, we create space for a deeper alignment to occur and we can move further into our purpose.

Pay as much attention to who you and
others are being as to what you are doing.

Keith had been a supervisor for many years and had managed many different types of employees. But nobody was quite like Simon. When Simon first started his job, Keith was skeptical. Simon was disorganized, absent-minded, and made lots of mistakes. On the other hand, his heart was always in the right place.

160

When it came to volunteering for the annual food drive, employee picnic, or company event, Simon was always the first one to raise his hand. Keith had considered letting Simon go many times, but his enthusiasm and cheer were infectious, and somehow Keith could never do it.

Over time, Keith realized that Simon was an important part of the work culture. Simon made the workplace better for everyone, even though he wasn't the best at his daily tasks. Everyone was happier, more productive, and more invested in the company because of Simon's presence. Eventually Keith moved Simon into a position where he spent more time on company and team events, where Simon's being could shine.

In what ways is your "doing" defining who you are at work? In your personal life?

How are you "being" at work? At home? How do you want to be?

Who You Be?

Take time this week to make a list of the most important or influential people in your life right now—both personal and professional—and then answer the following questions: How do the people who know you personally see you differently than those who know you professionally? What is different? What feels true? What feels false or inauthentic? How is your "doing" tied to your personality in these relationships? How is your "being"? Notice if you feel consistency or inconsistency in the way others perceive you. What is this saying about you?

Key 17: Live Your Passion on Purpose

*Always remember, you have within you the
strength, the patience, and the passion to
reach for the stars and to change the world.*
Harriet Tubman

Passion is a natural state. Finding our passion comes as a result of paying attention to what brings us joy and then choosing activities that support and nurture our passion. We can recognize passion in others—for example, when we see the passion of a concert musician come alive through the music. Feeling happy, joyful, and in alignment with our sense of purpose are just a few indicators of when we are experiencing passion.

Living our passion doesn't mean that we are always doing everything for ourselves. Sometimes it means we are serving others. Remember the story about Sheila, who discovered that her purpose was to bring her cheerful self to meeting other people's needs. Living out our passion can bring gratitude and the experience of making a difference in the world.

Once we tap into our passions, we can look for opportunities to weave them into our personal and professional lives. There is a sense of purpose to our activities when we feel passionate about them—our actions come from the heart. When we start focusing our energy on the things we love, they come easier and more effortlessly over time.

Bringing passion to your life will help you maintain better balance and happiness in all that you do.

Susan always wanted to be a gourmet chef. When she was 12 years old, she saw a television program with Julia Child cooking an elaborate feast for a group of French dignitaries. Susan was hooked. In her high school and college years, Susan focused on academics, graduated from college with a degree in finance, and took a job as an accountant.

Susan became very successful in her career, but food was still her passion. Susan loved cooking for her family, but she dreamed of being a gourmet chef.

One day a group of Susan's co-workers were answering the question, "If you didn't have to worry about money, what would you do for work?" When it came to Susan's turn, she told them about her desire to be a chef. One of her co-workers mentioned that her friend was starting a part-time catering business and looking for someone to help with the cooking. She suggested that Susan contact her.

Within three months, Susan found herself cooking an elaborate feast for a group of local business women at a weekend retreat. Susan was able to keep her full-time job as an accountant, but also live out her passion to be an occasional gourmet chef.

Where is the passion in your work? In your personal life?

What would you do if you didn't have to earn a living? How can you bring that passion more fully into your life now?

Passion Pursuit

Take a moment to find your passion by asking yourself the following questions: "What do I really love to do? What have I done in the past that I was really good at?" Spend the week noticing or remembering what you love and why it matters, and then take the inquiry one step deeper and ask what these things have in common. What do they share? Often, that is where deeper passion lies.

Key 18: Manage the Leader Within

*If you seek to lead, invest at least 50% of your
time leading yourself—your own purpose,
ethics, principles, motivation, conduct.*
Dee Hock

We all take a position of leadership at some point in our lives. Managing other people requires a delicate balance. To effectively lead others, we must first learn to lead ourselves in healthy and balanced ways. Leading ourselves is about becoming aware of our strengths, talents, and gifts; aligning them with our deepest intentions and purpose; and activating that knowledge to support our own health and well-being.

Leaders create integrity that comes from transparency. Authentic leaders lead by example. To "walk the talk" means making our intentions and actions congruent. Leaders also learn from their mistakes, seeing problems as opportunities for growth and development. This newfound knowledge becomes wisdom as it is passed onto others.

By leading ourselves effectively, we can learn to lead others as a whole person: mind, body, and spirit. Leading from our head uses only our thoughts. Well-rounded leaders engage people's hearts and their intuition. When we have learned to glean the wisdom from our experiences, we can create opportunities to share our wisdom through mentoring and leading others.

**To become an effective leader of others, learn
to lead yourself in healthy and balanced ways.**

Ever since Sam joined a commercial design firm, he had had a spark within him that yearned to create and manage his own ideas. The first few years in his job, Sam learned aspects of the design business and built a solid portfolio.

He started developing good habits for building relationships, managing accounts, and collaborating with his boss and design team to ensure that their clients were always satisfied. After five years of being with the firm, Sam decided it was finally time to take the leap and go out on his own.

By actively engaging his thoughts, feelings, and intuition, Sam learned about his own personal leadership style and motivations. Money was important, but building solid relationships of trust and respect with his clients was what Sam valued most. By developing healthy habits that served him well—such as setting goals and timelines, returning client calls promptly, and collaborating with colleagues from his personal and professional networks, Sam was led to a better position with his clients and colleagues. Establishing these habits early in his career set the foundation for Sam to become a solid leader within his own design firm.

In what ways have you been leading yourself effectively? What are your strengths as a leader of others?

How is your self-leadership connected to the way you lead others? How are they different?

Practice What You Teach

This week, notice every time you give someone else advice or make a suggestion. Keep a list for a day or two. Then, try following each piece of advice you've given. What happens?

Key 19: Soften Your Stance

> *A man wrapped up in himself*
> *makes a very small bundle.*
> Benjamin Franklin

We are all naturally powerful beings. When we come into alignment with our passions, our willpower often takes over and encourages us to speak and move with determination. To *soften your stance* is to step back from our natural impulse to speak or act with force and either choose a gentler response or none at all.

Using force or power may show people that we know what we're talking about, but it can also elicit resistance. We can be assertive on the basis of our knowledge but still be sensitive to the information that we don't yet have. Softening your stance allows you to listen for what you don't yet know.

Our mind can move directly and aggressively on impulse, while our spirit moves gently and calmly on our intuition. When we soften our stance, we choose the path of least resistance. Choosing to "take the high road" can require extra patience and tolerance; however, considering the needs of someone else or sacrificing your ego for the greater good can be worth the effort.

> ***Soften your stance to give yourself and others an opportunity to connect fully.***

Jake had been living in China for only three months, but he already knew that his two-year contract with the language institute was going to be a challenge. Jake prided himself on getting things done quickly and efficiently. In China, however, he found a different pace and approach. Jake had been trying to convince the institute leadership that his new language program was, indeed, effective, but they didn't seem to budge. What was he doing wrong?

One day at lunch, Jake expressed his frustration with a co-worker who was native Chinese. After listening attentively, the co-worker looked at Jake and said, "It's push versus pull." Jake looked confused.

His co-worker went on to explain that in the United States, people tended to push their ideas, believing that their ideas are the right ones. In China, on the other hand, his friend said, it is best to suggest an idea and pull people into it—make it a collaborative process. If you soften your stance, earn people's trust, and gently pull them to you, you will be much more successful. Over the next six months, Jake worked hard on softening his stance, and his program was a success.

Where could you soften your stance? What might change if you did?

In what ways have you observed changes in the responses of others depending on your approach? Why is this important to recognize?

How's That Working For You?

Think of a current situation in your life where you are not getting the results you desire, and take a moment to answer the following questions: What is your intention (desired result)? How important is it that you get your result? What are you willing to give up or compromise in order to get it? What other perspectives have you considered? How might softening your stance get you the desired result or something even better? Sometimes, the approach we're taking to achieve something works for *us* but is not necessarily the best approach for all concerned.

Key 20: Work Smarter, Not Harder

> *The major work of the world is not done*
> *by geniuses. It is done by ordinary people,*
> *with balance in their lives, who have learned*
> *to work in an extraordinary manner.*
> Gordon B. Hinckley

What's hard work? You might think of physically demanding tasks, paying attention to excessive detail, or many weeks, months, and years of effort leading to a high-quality final product. Working harder can bring us desired results, but it can also keep us from recognizing unproductive effort, ineffective process, and poor habits.

Working smarter is learning to prioritize, plan, and focus our energies with meaningful intent. We can produce powerful results without exerting as much effort by thinking carefully through our predicaments, considering past experiences, and aligning ourselves with specific goals before taking action. Working smarter means knowing our limitations, developing healthy and effective boundaries, and learning to love and respect ourselves enough to grow from our experience.

Work smarter to your own and others' advantage.

Stacey had always found it challenging to balance her life. Between work, night school, and her family, she felt like she was always behind. In addition, her ADHD complicated her ability to multitask. It was her second year of school and she was so excited about getting her Bachelor's degree—a dream she had wanted to pursue since she graduated from high school 20 years ago. And now that her kids were in high school, her dream was possible, but her life was hectic.

Then one of her college classes changed her life. To complete her business degree, Stacey was required to take a basic project management class. In the class, they used project management software to organize, prioritize, and document class projects.

During class one night, Stacey had a "light bulb moment." If these tools work so well for managing tasks, budgets, and work, why couldn't she use these same tools to help manage her life? Within two weeks, Stacey had translated several of the project management tools into tools for her personal life. Her schedule felt more organized, her personal budget was on track, and she felt relief.

How might you work more efficiently in your job? At home?

In what ways could doing things differently help you work and live smarter in your personal life?

Start, Stop, Continue

Take a moment to list some of your "good" and "bad" habits. What are you doing that's working for you? What is not? What would you like to start doing differently? What are your intentions? Goals? Ideal situations? Now take a sheet of paper and make three columns: Start, Stop, Continue. Review your list and place each habit in one of the categories accordingly:

- **Start** = What you are neglecting or not doing (i.e., exercise regularly)

- **Stop** = What is unproductive, unhealthy, or painful (i.e., negative self-talk)

- **Continue** = What is productive, healthy, or helpful (i.e., making healthy food choices)

By taking the time to start, stop, and continue habits, you will have a better idea of how to reprioritize your energies to work and live smarter.

Key 21: Go With the Flow

> *It's not your work to make anything happen.*
> *It's your work to dream it and let it happen.*
> Abraham Hicks

Change is a constant in life. Change feels like it is happening *to* us, but change is happening *for* us. If we have courage to move with the change, we can go with the flow and become part of it.

Going with the flow is allowing the natural rhythm of the universe to work with us. A constant stream of well-being is always flowing to us and through us. Going with the flow lets us release resistance, relax, and go with the current. Allowing teaches us to accept all things, including people, as they are right now, knowing that all things change with time.

To go with the flow requires patience and understanding. Through letting go, we can be both present and curious about the unknown and learn to develop a higher tolerance for ambiguity, trusting that everything we need to know and learn will be put in our path. When things don't come quickly or easily to us, we can choose to honor the timing of all things, and add wishes to our "waiting patiently list."

> ***Being able to practice allowing and acceptance***
> ***will help you learn how to go with the flow.***

Tammy was not happy. Why did they need to replace the order entry system? It had been working fine for years. She couldn't believe she had to learn a whole new system. She had been doing the same job for over 15 years and she knew the system better than anyone. Why go through all of this change? But it was inevitable. The company had decided that in order to meet their projected growth over the next five years, they needed to upgrade all of their software systems including the order entry system.

When the trainer arrived for the first day of a two-week training session, Tammy expressed her frustration by sitting stiffly back in her chair with her arms crossed through the entire morning session. At the lunch break, the trainer listened attentively as Tammy told him why she was unhappy. Then, he asked Tammy if he could show her a few things on the new system. After only 15 minutes of working together, Tammy was finally able to let go of her fear. By the next day of training she wasn't so angry, and at the end of the two weeks of training, Tammy was the star student!

In which areas of your life are you allowing or resisting? Of your work?

How might you let go and go with the flow? What would you be risking? What might change?

Flip It

Many of us compare our emotional state to that of a roller coaster—we say we're feeling "up" or "down." This week, try flipping it: instead of using vertical orientation—up and down, use horizontal—out and in. Feeling happy might feel expanded like breathing out, while feeling unhappy might feel compressed like holding in your breath. Feeling expanded or compressed carries less judgment than up or down and is not as dramatic as a roller coaster. That, in itself, is a more balanced and gentle approach to understanding emotions. Besides, this perspective allows you to exhale and let go.

Closing

The best and safest thing is to keep a balance in your life,
acknowledge the great powers around us and in us.
Euripides

Now that you've read each of the themes, answered the questions, and performed the activities, I encourage you to apply what you've learned to help bring better balance to your career, relationships, and life. At any time, you can create a new Balance Plan to help shift any aspect of your life as you choose. Remember: The power to make changes in your life is *always* in your hands.

My challenge to you is to see yourself as a whole person, to strengthen and nurture your new and existing relationships, and to believe that your gifts and talents were made to be shared with the world. Keep trying new things, eating new foods, listening to new music, and seeking to replace fear of the unknown with a curiosity of it. Once you realize that life is truly about the adventure of creating yourself, you will be able to live in the present moment more peacefully and joyfully than ever before—regardless of your circumstances.

I believe in you, and I believe you can make anything happen. Focus on what you truly desire. Be brave. Be bold. Savor the moments and memories with those around you. Live life to its fullest, and believe that your life has meaning and purpose. And remember, along your journey, to keep applying what you learn about yourself and others to experience better balance in your life.

About the Author

Michael Thomas Sunnarborg is an educator, author, and life coach. He has spent much of his life traveling and living in different parts of the world including Europe, Asia, and the South Pacific, and his travel blogs and photo galleries have been followed by thousands of readers worldwide. Michael currently resides in Minneapolis, Minnesota.

For information on coaching, presentations, and workshops given by Michael Thomas Sunnarborg, visit michaelsunnarborg.com

Other books by Michael Thomas Sunnarborg:

21 Days, Steps & Keys Workbook

21 Keys to Work/Life Balance:
Unlock Your Full Potential

21 Keys to Work/Life Balance Workbook

21 Steps to Better Relationships:
Find More Balance with Others

21 Steps to Better Relationships Workbook

21 Days to Better Balance:
Find More Balance in a Busy World

21 Days to Better Balance Workbook

Inspiration from the World

Order additional copies of this book,
eBook, and workbook at: 21complete.com

Follow on social media at:
Twitter: @21daystobalance
Blogger: blog.21daystobetterbalance.com
Facebook: 21daystobetterbalance

Acknowledgements

These books would not have been possible
without the help of some very special people.

A very special thank you to:

Tom & Yvonne Sunnarborg

Love and support from:

Becky, Jim, Nicolette & Natalie Wontor,
Dorothy Navarro, Shawn Boyd, Heike Peters,
Mary Texer, Robert Holloway, Saundra Halgrimson,
Pat Reynolds, and Arlan

Inspiration from:

Kathleen Blanc, Sheila Feigin, Honoree Corder,
Ann E. Boyum, Laura Ventrella, Sandra Beckwith,
Grant Harshbarger, Karen Bradley, Jerry & Esther Hicks and
Abraham, the music of Schiller, Altus, Rachmaninov,
Enigma, The Minnesota Symphony, Lisa Gerrard, and Enya

Friendship from:

Lukas J. Dickie, Jake Jones, Bob Manning,
Ryan Engelhardt, Matthias Potthoff, Rob Reitz,
Joe Kestel, Thomas O. Haakenson, Wyatt A. Spielman,
Joshua Avery, Jill Retzer, Chad Tearle, David Mann,
Jon Sharratt, Rick Gorman, Kathy Messerli, Kevin Reilly,
Matthew Singer, Blaine McGuire, Wayne Isaac Riddle,
Jim Weeks, Sally Mason, Stephen Carey, Dan Willie,
Jeff March, William W. Smith, and Becca Fuhrman

My favorite writing spaces:

The CW Central, Loft & North Pole, Caribou Coffee,
Starbucks, Barnes & Noble, Wilde Roast, Dunn Bros,
The Cabin Bemidji, and Blytheville

Spaces of silence and solitude compliments of:

The Green Hornet and The White Falcon

Namaste

Made in the USA
Middletown, DE
05 September 2015